Echoes from Down Under

BY MICHAEL CULLEN

Echoes from Down Under is an Irishman's collection of stories and anecdotes from his time living in Australia in the late 1980s. Tales of friendship, adventure, joy, and tragedy. Michael Cullen recounts his experiences as a newspaper journalist covering the courts in the Northern Territory.

He writes about drama on the high seas, the plight of Australia's First Nations' people, the wars fought at home and abroad, and the growing impact of climate change on the country. He interviews the redoubtable Clive James in Perth. He also recalls events from his days Down Under with throwbacks to his life in Ireland.

The book was inspired by real people and events and enlivened with literary flourish from the deep recesses of the author's mind. Some names were changed to protect identities. Artificial intelligence played no part in the composition of this book.

Published in 2024 by Gregmar Books
1 Albert Park, Sandycove, Co Dublin, Ireland A96 XD63
Email: mgmcullen@gmail.com

ISBN 9798324002138

Limited edition copy

Copyright. Echoes from Down Under, May 2024

All rights reserved.

No part of this publication may be reproduced,
stored in a retrieval system, or transmitted,
in any form, or by any means, without the
prior written submission of the author.

Cover design by Claire Foley, Dynamo

For Liam and Gill

Contents

Acknowledgements
Introduction
Foreword

Chapter 1	Innocence Disturbed
Chapter 2	Off to Kakadu
Chapter 3	Stranded in Rome
Chapter 4	Shocking News
Chapter 5	A Move North
Chapter 6	Gentle as a Dove
Chapter 7	Somewhere to Hide
Chapter 8	Living the Laugh
Chapter 9	Hunter Gatherer
Chapter 10	Plagued by Violence
Chapter 11	Call to Arms
Chapter 12	Football Crazy
Chapter 13	Titan of Wit
Chapter 14	Mercurial Artist
Chapter 15	Man, Overboard Portside!
Chapter 16	Coasting It
Chapter 17	Great Scott
Chapter 18	Gutsy Pom
Chapter 19	Hollywood Starlet
Chapter 20	Home Again
Chapter 21	Helga Phones
Chapter 22	Wrongly Accused
Chapter 23	Fond Farewell
Chapter 24	Uncharted Waters
Chapter 25	Australia's Own
Chapter 26	A Year in Bondi

Acknowledgements

The Irish Times; *Business Post*; British Broadcasting Corporation (BBC) – 'The Great Australian Railway Journeys'; *The West Australian*; *Sydney Morning Herald*, Australian Broadcasting Corporation (ABC); *Australian Financial Review*; *The Rise and Fall of Alan Bond* by Paul Barry; *Katherine Advertiser*; Julia Cullen; Jenny Cullen; Declan Flood; Padraic Regan; Cyril Byrne; Enda O'Coineen; Jamie Helly; John Fanning; Sean Boyle; Breandán O'Broin; Breda Brown; Fremantle Sailing Club; Japingka Aboriginal Art in Fremantle; Western Australian Tourism Commission; Rottnest Island Authority; Tourism NT; Australian Embassy Dublin; Raidio Teilifís Éireann (RTÉ); Emma Horgan; Antoinette O'Callaghan.

Introduction

"The very remoteness kindles the imagination of the adventurous hunter" – Fred Bear

Western Australia is remarkably parochial, which given its geographical isolation is no surprise. The State capital Perth is said to be the world's remotest city. In terms of distance, it is further away from any other conurbation in Australia and beyond. Known as the 'City of Light', it is 1,200 miles from Adelaide and almost 2,500 miles from Sydney.

WA accounts for one third of the entire land mass of Australia. The state is the size of Western Europe with space enough to accommodate thirty-seven countries measuring the length and breadth of Ireland. Its population density is one person per square kilometre. Compare that to Ireland's 72 people per square kilometre.

It has seven climate zones and six deserts - its Little Sandy Desert is one and a half times bigger than Ireland. Over 90 per cent of WA's population live within 30 miles of the ocean.

Aeroplanes brought closure to the tyranny of distance. Katherine lies inland in the heart of the Northern Territory, 310 kilometres south of Darwin. Nestled in a land of scorched earth and scrub, it's where the outback meets the tropics. The dry season runs from April to November, when hardly a cloud veils the gold of the sun. The wet season runs for the remaining months with heavy downpours and high humidity, particularly during the build-up.

Foreword

"There's no friend as loyal as a book" –
Ernest Hemingway

EM Forster, author of *A Room with a View*, once observed: "Long books, when read, are usually overpraised, because the reader wishes to convince himself and others that he has not wasted his time." British novelist Hilary Mantel's advice to writers was that you should try to mean what you say when writing a book – that is, try not to say what you don't mean.

Anne Lamott, author of *Bird by Bird*, has lessons on how to become a writer. She said writing a novel is like driving a car at night; you can only see as far as your headlights, but you can make the whole trip that way. It's a wonderful metaphor for writing, and for life.

In writing a book, editing is said to be the hidden secret of great work. At the end of the last century, bestselling author Stephen King admonished: "Kill your darlings, kill your darlings, even when it breaks your egocentric little scribbler's heart." My apologies in advance. If only I had more self-discipline.

American-British novelist Henry James had a guiding principle about writing, which is worth noting. He said: "To be interesting in one beautiful sentence after another. To be interesting; not to change the world."

Country singer Willie Nelson's take on being an author: "They say that writing the first line of a book is the hardest. Thank God that's over."

Chapter 1

Innocence Disturbed

"I hurt myself today, to see if I still feel; I focus on the pain, the only thing that's real" -
The Hurt, a song written by Trent Reznor, released by Nine Inch Nails, and reimagined by Johnny Cash

Katherine, November 1988

The door flew open the way dynamite opens a safe, followed by the soft shuffle of a poorly hung fly screen skimming across the kitchen floor. A young man breezed in with a grin wider than Katherine Gorge. Phil Shaw was irreducibly Australian. "G'day Mike," he said cheerfully as he landed a gentle fist on my shoulder. "How's it goin' mate?"

"All good," I replied nonchalantly, "and you?" "Bonzer!" he thundered, intimating that the world hadn't been too unjust to him that day. "Did you get the football results?" I asked him, half-suspecting that other events from his Sunday shift at the *Katherine Advertiser* had proved a distraction - not least his habit of flirting with Lucy in production.

"Ah, silly me, it went clear out of my head," Phil said. "Susie and Alex didn't show up today, so I was busier than a croc harvesting Japanese tourists. Sorry mate. Tell you one thing, I'm famished!" He opened the fridge door and reached for a packet of Tim Tam chocolate biscuits.

"Whatya know?" he asked, "any gossip?" I reminded him that he should be the one with all the news. It was then that I noticed his left arm was in a sling. How would he explain that? It couldn't be from playing sport as Phil would run a mile from anything demanding physical exertion.

His inertness didn't stop him from having a profound knowledge of Test cricket. Whenever Australia played England in the Ashes he was glued to the TV. Phil liked to try and impress people by reciting lines from Francis Thompson's poem, 'At Lords': *For the field is full of shades as I near the shadowy coast/And a ghostly batsman plays to the bowling of a ghost.*

He'd wax lyrical about his all-time hero, the record-breaking Australian batsman Don Bradman, reminding me that from 1928 to 1948 'The Don' managed to score an average of 99.94 runs per innings in Test cricket. In 1948, Bradman's Invincibles won an Ashes series four-nil in England, partly due to an experimental rule that allowed for a new ball every 55 six-ball overs.

When watching cricket on TV, he'd sing 'Howzat', a 1976 chart hit for the Australian band Sherbet. Sweet divine! The saccharine-fuelled tune became a cricket anthem sung loudly by ground organisers at limited-overs matches. Howzat is what cricketers the world over shout out when appealing to the umpire for a wicket.

Despite his sedentary lifestyle, Phil was agile. Using his bear-like frame he could lift sizeable weights at the gym with little effort, yet he struggled in a swimming pool or on a tennis court. He suffered from migraines and dizzy spells, which dimmed his concentration. He developed epilepsy and was on daily medication to head off seizures.

Apart from watching cricket on TV, he liked to place the odd wager. When it came to horse racing, he knew the code, the signals, and the terms of engagement. Three o'clock on the afternoon of the first Tuesday in November meant more to him than all his birthdays and Christmases combined. It's when the whole of Australia comes to a standstill for the Melbourne Cup.

On his days off, Phil would go fishing. At night, he'd stretch out on the couch with his Walkman on and sing along to John Williamson's 'True Blue'. Shortly after, he'd be sound asleep and snoring. On one of his bedroom walls was a poster of Annie Lennox performing at the Sydney Opera House. Facing it was a print of Keith Haring's painting of Grace Jones, naked apart from white scribbles all over her body.

He handed me a cup of coffee strong enough to trot a mouse and proceeded to explain to me the cause of his injured arm. Three days earlier, he had headed off on a bush excursion, driving over 300 kilometres to Kakadu National Park in his Toyota utility, or - as the Aussies prefer to call it - a 'ute'.

Off-roads in the Top End can be tricky at the best of times, but when the dry season's clear blue skies give way to the wet season build-up, things turn decidedly dodgy. Tropical weather conditions take hold from November to April.

Some people find the humidity disturbing, and they lose their mental composure; they go 'troppo'. The wet season transforms the upper crust of the Territory's baked earth parched by months of sunlight. Rising temperatures usher in monsoon rains. Heavy raindrops perform a tap dance that bathes the land. The air is saturated by the sweet scent of petrichor. In a scene reminiscent of a David Attenborough documentary on the Serengeti, a metamorphosis occurs where a green, lush, and flooded panorama springs to life.

It was after a heavy downpour that Phil's accident struck. His vehicle lost traction on a bridge crossing and crashed head-on into the bank opposite. He had no chance of bracing himself for impact. It's just as well he had his seatbelt on, and the front of the ute was fitted with bull bars, otherwise his injuries may well have been more serious. He'd obviously missed the luminous orange 'Road Unsafe When Under Water' warning signs.

He managed to escape from the prang with a dislocated shoulder and a few gashes and bruises on his limbs. That was it; he was dead fortunate. His old jalopy got off lightly too, with just a shattered windscreen and dents to the roof which a saucepan of boiling water and a plunger could remedy.

"Fancy heading to Kakadu at the weekend?" Phil asked shamelessly. "We're both off work, and I lose the sling tomorrow. Let's check the forecast on Friday. Unless there's a storm brewing, we'll go for it, yeah? Mike, you need to get out of town more. It'll do your head in."

To say I was taken aback by his zeal was an understatement. He'd got away with one, and he knew it. He was being brazen and the gambler in him fancied another punt. With so many dark clouds on the horizon, would we be pushing our luck?

Phil sensed my unease. As they say, anxiety is like being the only person that knows the world is ending but everyone else calls crazy. Either way, the two of us decided that the best course of action would be to hold off on making a call until Friday, at which time we'd have a good take on the weekend's weather.

Phew! If my beloved mother back in Ireland knew that I'd planned to head into the bush at the start of the cyclone season, she'd have been at her wits end. She'd tell me that I'd lost my mind, while, at the same time, masking her unconditional love for her youngest offspring.

Phil was a genial character who smiled a lot. His diffidence meant he had little to say to strangers. But when he was in a talkative mood, he shielded his true self by telling corny one-liners. He gave off an air of innocence and vulnerability which most people he met found endearing.

He could play a blinder in chatting up a girl in a bar or at a party, but he was happier biding his time, "getting to know her". He found any form of confrontation hostile. He thrived on the isolation of his fishing trips and sorting out the tackle with his Swiss Army knife.

However, not everyone is what they appear to be, and so it was with Phil.

One evening after work, we were chilling on the porch with a carton of VB, when the movement of a monitor lizard in the garden unsettled us. He jumped from his seat and rushed down the stairs to help the stricken reptile. He cleared an area of debris, allowing the lizard to scurry through a hole in the border fence. He then returned upstairs.

He sat down and pivoted his chair. A pall of urgency clouded his eyes. He said that he had something to tell me - in confidence. He reached into his pocket and pulled out a wallet, sifting through the flaps.

Handing me a photograph, he said the woman holding the young boy in her arms was his mother, Laura. The photo was taken when he was six years old.

Phil then proceeded to unspool his story.

Innocence Disturbed

It was a mild, winter afternoon in a suburb of Hobart. The year was 1968. Phil was at home on the couch watching cartoons on television. Beams from the low-lying winter sun filtered through the window blinds. His mother was in the kitchen fixing a snack for her son.

She spread Vegemite on toast and put a generous slice of lamington sponge cake on a plate, along with a glass of Milo chocolate milk. She carried the cushion-bottomed tray into the sitting room and placed it softly on Phil's lap. He looked up at her with a feeling of joy. She beamed back at him adoringly.

She gave her only child a peck on the cheek and gently rubbed his head. Phil chuckled at Daffy Duck's antics on *Looney Tunes*. His mother walked towards a wooden cabinet, on top of which rested a china vase and a framed family photo. She opened a drawer and reached inside. She then quietly left the room, clutching something in her right hand.

A moment or two later, and a sharp bang rang out. At first, Phil thought it was the cartoons on the TV. He sprung up from the couch and the tray littered the ground. He rushed into the hall. From the doorway, he could see his mother. She lay stretched on her back on the kitchen floor, blood pooled around her head, her slender body motionless.

As Phil moved closer, he met her open eyes fixed on the ceiling. Part of her face was obscured by strands of blood-stained, blonde hair. Phil leaned over and picked up the .38-calibre handgun resting next to her open hand. The weapon was warm at the grip.

Stunned and confused, he stared at the barrel. His next-door neighbour stormed through the back door into the kitchen. She took the boy into her arms in a desperate effort to conceal the horror. The scene turned to chaos as emergency service crews crowded the house.

A few days later, Phil and his neighbour returned to his home to retrieve his personal belongings. He recalled the two of them walking slowly together in the hallway, surrounded by a hollow silence and the pungent tang of bleach. From that moment on, swimming lessons and the smell of chlorine was a reminder of his dread.

Phil's mother had a history of mental health problems. Her doctor prescribed all manner of medication to help her cope. After drinking bouts, she would take to her bed in the afternoon, often not resurfacing until the next morning. She suffered hallucinations from delirium tremens – the DTs - the severest form of alcohol withdrawal.

Being an only child, Phil was able to wheedle and get his way, but when his mother was at her lowest ebb she would suddenly flip and became a termagant. The ache he felt was visceral and there was no refuge. As John Steinbeck once wrote: "There are some among us who live in rooms of experience that we can never enter".

To help pay household bills, Phil's mother worked part-time as a secretary in a law firm. Phil's father, George, quit the family home when his son was three years old, leaving no trace of his whereabouts. In *The Interpretation of Dreams*, Sigmund Freud described the death of a father as "the most important event, the most poignant loss, of a man's life".

To lose a mother in childhood in such horrific circumstances can be a catalyst for all manner of damage; to lose both parents at such an early age is crushing. Too young to articulate the hurt, the fallout often manifests itself years after the fact. Suicide creates an enigma, challenging those left behind to join the dots.

In his early teens, Phil discovered that his dad was a jackaroo on a cattle station. He later moved to Coonamble in New South Wales where he worked on a wheat farm. He remarried a much younger woman named Maggie. Phil seemingly had a half-brother, with whom he had no contact.

Shortly after his mother's death, Phil was taken into foster care until such time as he could be formally adopted by his Aunt Kate and her family in Melbourne. He was happy there and loved growing up with his two cousins. He remembered his Uncle Bill picking him up and sitting him on his shoulders. It became his favourite place to be as a child.

Phil attended a non-denominational school where he was an unscholarly student. His uncle was appalled by the Catholic Church after several of his classmates were abused by priests during their time boarding in a school in Ballarat, the goldrush city located about 100 kilometres from Melbourne.

He believed the clergy should have no role in the education system. In his opinion, it was a church that valued the obedience they demanded from young children for the clerical collar higher than learning and the love of God.

The Australian Royal Commission on Institutional Responses to Child Sexual Abuse, which made its final report abuse in December 2017, said that both the Christian Brothers and diocesan clergy in Ballarat were engaged in the systematic sexual abuse of young boys over a long period of time.

Those who tried to raise the issue of clerical abuse in public and challenge the Catholic Church's authority were met with the response that became familiar the world over - the complete denial of survivors' testimonies, the safeguarding of perpetrators, evasion, lies and cover-up.

During his school years, Phil's diligence paid off. He passed his exams, at times securing A-grades. He wasn't your classroom swot – far from it - he just loathed and feared being bored. His studies kept him occupied and offered a distraction from his recurring misery.

He was immensely grateful to his relatives in Melbourne for the love, help and support they gave him at such a critical stage in his life. The family kept in contact by phone. They exchanged birthday and Christmas cards and met up every second year.

At the age of 19, Phil sought professional counselling. The psychiatrist told him that he had post-traumatic stress disorder (PTSD), which came as no surprise given the cataclysmic event he witnessed as a boy. While the memories he stored could never be erased, he was told that his trauma may lessen over time. It wasn't possible to be any more certain.

Every day was a mountain climb with steep demands. Undaunted, Phil recognised his task - keep breathing, hold on to the life he was given and the life he was still birthing. He took strength from valuing his desires, joys, and sorrows. He knew he had to muster courage and explore by saying yes to the unfolding of his own journey.

All he could do was make peace with the unpredictability that lay ahead. There were days when Phil had "catastrophic thoughts", his mind a war zone. His voice lightened as he assured me that sharing his secret after so many years of locking it away was a relief.

On his days off, Phil would throw on his 'Yeah, nah' say-nothing-when-you-don't-really-need to-say-anything tee-shirt, the flimsiest shorts he could find and a pair of flip flops - which Aussies call thongs. I informed him that elsewhere in the world a thong was a toothpick cover for the body's nether regions. He fell about laughing.

Once fed and watered, he'd hop into his ute and drive off to the bush, an oasis from the world and a refuge from his torment; at least until the next nightmare struck when he would awaken in a sweat, screaming at the imagined blast of gunfire, the whiff of cordite and the panic swirling in his head.

Not surprisingly, Phil found it hard to sleep. On quiet, still nights, he'd sit out on the porch on his own, smoking weed and counting the stars. His inner pain recalled a line Harper Lee, author of *To Kill a Mockingbird*, once wrote: "We never truly understand another person until we see things from their point of view."

In the coming days, the rains came and passing clouds burst with extreme prejudice, signalling change. Our fortunes, however, were about to improve. On the Friday, ABC Radio in Darwin reported that the Top End was in for a respite.

Phil was ready. With the speed of a fleeing tiger beetle, he got the fishing rods out from under the bed. He brushed off the mounds of dry muck clung to his wellies.

While I would never claim to be a dab hand at fishing, the thought of landing a barramundi at a shaded billabong in Kakadu's floodplains stirred me. At the same time, the prospect of dropping a hook somewhere in the wide expanse of a tropical park that's home to 10,000 or so saltwater crocodiles was a tad ominous.

As well as worrying about Phil's damaged arm, the thought of embarking on a 600-kilometre round trip in an old ute played on my mind. Fingers crossed the air conditioning would be on its best behaviour and rattle into action on our drive along the Stuart Highway to Arnhem Land - an expanse which stretches north-east across 97,000 square kilometres - and is home to the Yolngu Aboriginal people.

Chapter 2

Off to Kakadu

"I wanna know, have you ever seen the rain? Comin' down on a sunny day" – Creedence Clearwater Revival

Katherine, November 1988

Phil's alarm went off at 6am. After we had shaved and showered, we grabbed a quick coffee and a bowl of Weet-Bix. We were ready for our big adventure in Kakadu. Everything needed for the day's fishing had been packed in the back of the ute the night before. As we drove out of town, we stopped for fuel and soft drinks for the esky.

We were soon bouncing along the road. We were like two youngsters about to experience the thrill of their first trip to Disneyland. It was too early in the day for spinning yarns and telling jokes, so I pressed Talking Heads' Little Creatures into the tape deck, and we lost ourselves in 'Road to Nowhere'.

The Stuart Highway runs for 2,700 kilometres from Port Augusta in South Australia, all the way up to Darwin and the fringes of the Timor Sea. It's also known as the Explorer Highway and The Bitumen. It was named after Scottish explorer John McDouall Stuart, the first European to travel across Australia from south to north.

Stops along the way include the world's opal capital Coober Pedy, Alice Springs, Tennant Creek, and Katherine. Alice Springs, or Alice as it's affectionately known, has a population of 25,000, one in five of whom are Indigenous.

Located near the centre of Australia, it is the outback town closest to Uluru, home to Ayers Rock, which the Aboriginals treasure as an ancient sacred resting ground. The 17-hour drive from Uluru to Katherine runs through the heart of middle Australia.

Coober Pedy is an intriguing place. A small mining town 1,870 kilometres south of Katherine, it is known as the opal capital of the world. In summer, temperatures regularly hit 52 degrees Celcius. In such extreme conditions, electronic equipment must be stored in refrigerators. Birds have been known to fall out of the sky.

The words 'coober pedy' translate from the local Aboriginal language as 'white man in a hole'. More than half of its residents live underground in 150 subterranean homes, hotels and guesthouses dug into iron-rich sandstone and siltstone rock under the town. It was the location for George Miller's 1985 blockbuster, *Mad Max – Beyond Thunderdome*, starring Mel Gibson and Tina Turner.

The Stuart Highway is the only road in Australia with no speed limit, prompting motorists to drive with abandon. It explains the high rate of animal kill as fast-moving road trains, pulling two or more trailers, haul goods from the south to townships and communities across the Northern Territory.

Commuting by road from South Australia to the Territory had long been an ordeal. The highway was a series of mud tracks linking homesteads in the bush. It was why so many people commuted from Adelaide to Darwin by train.

In 1878, the first railway tracks were laid to connect the continent. The job wasn't completed until this century – many cathedrals were built faster.

Operated by Journey Beyond Rail Expeditions and first known as The Afghan Express, The Ghan was described as one of the world's great passenger trains. Its scheduled travelling time, including extended stops for passengers to do off-train tours along the 2,979-kilometre stretch of land, was 53 hours 15 minutes.

In 1979, South Australia's State government, with support from the Federal parliament in Canberra, gave the go ahead for a sealed road to the Territory. In 1987, the Stuart Highway was completed at a cost of $140 million.

The never-ending and repetitive roadside landscape of red soil and scrub dominates the 150-kilometre stretch of highway from Katherine to South Alligator River. The monotony is in stark contrast to Kakadu's towering beauty.

The 20,000-square kilometre park dates back 65,000 years to Aboriginal Dreamtime. It was the traditional home of the Bininj and Mungguy people, who lived there for tens of thousands of years. Nowadays, they jointly manage it with Parks Australia.

While the name Kakadu may sound Aboriginal, it is in fact the western misinterpretation of a language spoken by local Indigenous communities.

Savanna woodlands and lowlands account for about 80 per cent of the park. It is home to 2,000 plant species, around one-third of all Australian bird species and about one-fifth of all the country's mammals. As a result, it's no surprise to learn that Kakadu is one of 20 Unesco World Heritage listed sites in Australia.

Waterfalls and plunge pools abound in this untrammelled land. Where bodies of water once flowed, there are now jaw-dropping escarpments with beige and red-streaked chiselled rock stretching skywards. Tourists get glimpses of some of Australia's best-known wildlife, including kangaroo, koala, dingo, and buffalo.

The park's three Alligator Rivers - South, East and West - were named by the coastal explorer Phillip Parker King, who, in 1920, wrongly assumed the reptiles he spotted were alligators. Little did he know at the time that alligators' snouts are wide, rounded, and u-shaped, while crocodiles have long, pointed, v-shaped jaws.

The alligator, synonymous with the Florida Everglades, has a wide upper jaw, which allows for its teeth to remain hidden in its mouth. Gators are more like the freshwater croc native to Australia. Largely tame and shy, a gator will rarely attack people, unless, like a rat when cornered, it defends itself. The same can be said for the black caiman endemic to South America.

Reptile experts says the chance of a person being attacked by a gator is one in three million. 2001 and 2006 had the most fatalities, with three people in Florida dying in each of those years.

There were only 23 fatal attacks from 1948 to 2016. There are around 200,000 gators in the Everglades, but over 1.5 million in the state of Florida, living in natural and man-made freshwater lakes, ponds, rivers, and wetlands.

Phil and I were headed for the South Alligator, located about 200 kilometres east of Darwin. It is one of Top End's rivers richest in barramundi. 'Barra' is a type of sea bass - tasty, chewy, and nutritious.

The river allows tourists year-round access through sealed roads and concrete boat ramps. The tropical summer and run-off months produce the best catch. At other times of the year, anglers go reef fishing out from the river's mouth in search of black jewfish and golden snapper.

Aware of the perils of fishing in Kakadu, we convinced ourselves that we'd be okay during the heat of the day when the crocs stay submerged. The best time to spot a croc during the build-up to the wet season is sunrise and sunset. Once the monsoons take hold, they disperse as the wetlands flood. It's when Katherine Gorge becomes an unsafe place to swim with an influx of saltwater crocodiles.

Salties plane along the water's surface, either slow drifting or swimming at about 10 kilometres per hour, powered by a thrashing tail. Their movement appears simultaneously insouciant and graceful. But like the proverbial swan, below the waterline they paddle away like billy-o.

While a croc's body doesn't allow them to jump high off the ground, once they are in the water their muscular tail can propel them up to eight feet in the air, which includes the length of their bodies.

It allows them to lunge at prey in a surprise attack. Despite having short, stubby legs, which help them steer underwater, a croc can outrun a human on land. In the water, they move at warp speed: "Down by the river, in the heat of the day, the crocodile sleeps and awaits its prey."

Bright yellow warning signs and the word danger written in red capitals remind visitors to be 'crocwise' as 'Crocodiles inhabit this area' and 'Attacks cause injury or death'. What's more: 'Do not enter the water', 'Keep away from the water's edge', 'Do not clean fish near the water's edge' and 'Remove all fish and food waste from the banks'.

The warning notices are dotted throughout the park, but that doesn't deter tourists from taking chances. It's a crazy gamble. An attack by the world's largest reptile spells trouble. Big trouble. Should a croc get a firm grip and spin its victim's torso around in what is called the death roll, the outcome is usually grim.

The roll helps compensate for the croc's small stomach - the size of a basketball - enabling the animal to tear small pieces of flesh off a larger carcass. It's worth noting that they have a modest appetite and can only consume so much food at one time. Two average-sized dogs would keep an adult croc fed for a year.

The croc hides its prey in its nest or in a mangrove. There are differing views as to why it does this. Australian reptile experts believe that it may not be because they prefer rotting flesh. A decomposing carcass will attract scavengers, such as turtles and mud crabs, which are themselves fresh food for the croc, thereby creating a domino effect.

Before 1971, the year when saltwater crocodiles were declared a protected species in the Northern Territory, they were hunted close to extinction. Since then, numbers in the Top End have increased exponentially, from about 3,000 to a whopping 100,000-plus in the wild.

The renowned TV crocodile hunter and zookeeper Steve Irwin, who died tragically after being pierced by a stingray barb while filming off Queensland's Great Barrier Reef, once said that it may surprise people to learn that crocs are romantic and passionate lovers - "it's not wham-bam, thank you ma'am", he remarked with a depthless knowledge of his subject. Irwin based his findings on behaviours he observed in crocodile parks in northern Australian.

There's a crocodile tale told by a member of the Aboriginal Badmardi community. "In the creation era, a man and his wife were hunting for turtle in an escarpment pool, and the man was killed by Kinga, the first crocodile. When the woman saw his floating intestines, she knew her husband was dead. Kinga went down to the lowlands to live in the rivers and waterholes of the floodplains, and Modjarrki, the smaller freshwater crocodile, remained in the pools. Today, when crocodiles are opened, their intestines resemble the skull of the man killed."

After we had spent around three hours fishing at the billabong, it began to rain, softly at first. It didn't bother us greatly, and we soaked up its coolness. Phil managed to catch four barramundi and I lured two on the hook, but one escaped after my line got entangled in weed. Our feats made us feel happier than a drift of pigs gorging on swill.

As Phil came towards me whistling Johnnie Ray's 'Just Walking in the Rain', there was a loud crack of thunder. The drizzle soon turned to a deluge. Then, with lightning speed, all hell broke loose. Neither of us could have guessed the chaos that was set to unfold.

It began with the screech of a car, breaking and skidding to a halt on the opposite riverbank. A man in uniform jumped out of the vehicle. With one hand resting on the steering wheel, he began hooting the horn and shouting at us. He became hysterical and yelled out a stream of invective.

It was bedlam.

"What are you guys doin'?" Get your asses over here quick smart!" Phil and I didn't dawdle. We pulled off our boots, flung them into the back of the car and legged it. We made it to the opposite bank, where shade was a fleeting commodity. The ranger stood motionless, fury flooding his veins. He removed his hat and fanned himself.

Straightening his stance to stress the severity of his intent, he stared at us, stone silent. When eventually he found the words to speak, he said that only "complete dills" hung out at a billabong with so many salties nearby. There were safe viewing platforms at Cahill's Crossing and Yellow Water, both within an hour's drive.

"Who are you guys, anyway?" he asked, sharply. Phil gave him our names and said that we'd driven from Katherine that morning. "And where do you work?" The *Katherine Advertiser,* Phil replied. "Struth!" he cried. "Luigi's a mate of mine." He meant Luigi Albano, our boss.

Off to Kakadu

"My name's Warren, Warren Boyd," he said in his best outback impression of James Bond. "You might have guessed from my getup, I'm a park ranger here. Well, I reckon, even after that kick in the guts, it's good to meet you blokes."

Phil apologised for the ruction. He assured Warren that we were at the billabong to fish. No other reason. Unlike many visitors to Kakadu, croc sightings were of no interest to us. We said that we were aware from working at the newspaper about the attacks on tourists, some of whom end up eviscerated.

Warren answered with a look that indicated Groundhog Day. A week before, a ranger answered an emergency call after two Swedish visitors got too close to a croc nesting in a riverbank. The couple scurried up a tree. They were lucky as such a gambit is no guarantee of safety. Crocs can jump several feet in the air. And they are patient beasts, content to wait.

More drama then unfolded. Warren anxiously pressed a finger to his lips, urging silence. He gestured for us to get down on our knees and remain as still as a statue. The water's surface rippled as we lay crouched beneath the trees. At a guess, the croc heading our way measured about four metres in length. It looked ginormous.

The square patch beyond its eyes showed above the water as it rested near the surface. Did it spot us? Were we in danger? Could it be the same nesting croc that scared the daylights out of the Swedish couple a week before? Seconds later, and there was a hush.

The billabong was still as a pond. We stayed in the same spot for a while longer. Once we felt it was safe enough to move, Warren offered to drive us over to the bank where we had been fishing. We kept a watchful eye out for any further menace and hurriedly gathered up our belongings. The esky's ice cubes were struggling against time and temperature to keep our catch of the day fresh.

As we got into the ute, Phil thanked Warren for all his help. "No worries, it comes with the territory," he replied, outwardly oblivious to the pun. "Make sure to tell Luigi Wombat sends his regards," he added.

Wombat? That got me scratching my head.

Why on earth would anyone confuse Warren with one of Australia's most cherished marsupials? He didn't have teeth that never stopped growing. Surely not for using his rear end to defend himself. Given all he'd done to save our souls, the sobriquet had to be a salute to his reliability and patience.

It was four in the 'arvo', and we were tired and hungry. A couple of meat pies washed down with a can of flat Coke gave us a fighting chance. It had been a busy day. We now rested our hopes on a new plan of action.

Rather than return to Katherine, we decided it made more sense to travel on for 65 kilometres and overnight in Jabiru, a Kakadu township named after the black-necked stork.

Off to Kakadu

As we drove along the trail before cover of darkness, we were enthralled by the wildness and quietude. It was as if we were surrounded by ancient souls. The serenity was broken by the sound of a helicopter and distant gunfire. We later learned that it was park rangers on a buffalo cull.

Time for more Talking Heads. As 'Psycho Killer' played, Phil explained the song's origins. It was inspired by the 'Son of Sam' murders perpetrated by David Berkowitz in New York in 1975, which led to the city's biggest ever manhunt. The song, released shortly after Berkowitz's capture in 1977, combined pop rock with shrieking gibberish. David Byrne sang a bridge in French to create the delusion of a psychotic killer who imagined himself as refined for having the *nous* to speak a foreign language.

Rather than head to Jabiru, we continued for another hour to Ubirr, which is listed as a Unesco World Heritage site for its Aboriginal art. When we got there, we went on a 250-metre-high rock climb. It reminded me of the time in Ireland when I made the steep ascent up the stone steps at Skellig Michael in County Kerry.

At the peak in Ubirr, we were humbled by the vast landscape, a 360-degree panorama across the floodplains. We were in time to catch sight of one of the most sublime sunsets imaginable as the sky changed colour. The memory of such a mesmerising vision still triggers a dopamine hit and a skin full of goosebumps.

After our descent, we made tracks for the nearby Aurora Lodge. The barbequed fish they served up went down a treat. We retired for the night. Following hours of torrential rain, road closures forced the cancellation of our morning swim at Jim Jim Falls. Our stay in Kakadu was over, and it was time to return to Katherine.

Phil said that while he was relieved neither of us had ended up in a croc's jaws, a crazy part of him felt deflated. It was as if he was deprived of a once-in-a-lifetime wrestle with his would-be attacker! With about 30 kilometres to go, the ute ran out of fuel. Fortunately, we had filled up the jerry can before we left Katherine the previous day.

We got home before the heavens opened; our minds stimulated but our bodies aching. Everyone at the *Advertiser* heard about our escapade. With every tale shared, the fish we caught gained an inch or two in length. It was as if the three-year-old outsider that Phil backed in the Melbourne Cup was first to cross the finish line. And all we wanted was to celebrate with our mates in the winners' enclosure.

Chapter 3

Stranded in Rome

"The best-laid plans of mice and men, go often awry" –
Robert Burns

November 1987

Destination Perth, Western Australia

Wind back a year to November 1987. That's when my story starts. Australia Day loomed – *my* own personal Australia Day, that is. With goodbyes to family and friends said and suitcases packed, I was ready for my long-awaited departure with unfettered dreams.

The first leg on my marathon trip to Perth was a connecting flight from London, with fuel stops in Dubai, Bombay, and Singapore. From there, it was on to Melbourne. However, a short time before the plane was due to take off at Heathrow Airport the adventure turned into an ordeal. A bomb scare in Terminal Four delayed the flight for six hours.

Passengers bound for Melbourne were soon informed that the flight was cancelled. Alitalia, Italy's national carrier, decided that the best way of getting us to our destination as soon as possible – at the busiest time of year for flights from England to Down Under – was to fly to Rome, and from there on to Sydney.

As we prepared to land at Leonardo da Vinci-Fiumicino Airport, it dawned on me why Italy's capital was hailed as the Eternal City.

Although we were unaware of it at the time, we were about to spend the next four days there – which, at the time, felt frustrating. It was as if we were in a state of limbo.

In normal circumstances, most everyone would jump at the chance of a sojourn in Rome. Yet here we were on our way to the other side of the world with no indication as to when we might get there. Everything was, so to speak, up in the air. The airline put us up in a Holiday Inn close to the city centre.

It was 1987, a time before mobile phones and devices, and we were under curfew – under strict orders not to venture outside the hotel grounds lest we missed our flight call. We had to be prepared to leave the hotel for the airport at any moment, with little or no notice.

Other than that, the repeated response from the staff at our hotel over the coming days when we enquired about our departure was "we know nothing… *dopo*", which soon became clear to me was Italian for 'later'.

Forty or so airline passengers were stranded in one of the world's most amazing cities for goodness knows how long, and we were under orders to remain in our hotel the entire time! It was as if someone had gifted us a winning Lotto ticket, and - as the girl did in the TV ad – promptly grabbed it back.

By day three of our imposed confinement, people's patience had worn thin. That morning, I got talking to a fellow passenger, a Greek gentleman named Georgios. He suggested that we hire a taxi and set off on a fast-track tour of Rome. The curfew could wait.

Our first stop was the Baths of Caracalla, the city's second-largest public baths. Next up, the Colosseum. We were amazed by the number of feral cats that made their home among the ancient ruins of the once 85,000-capacity amphitheatre.

From the top of the Spanish Steps, the skyline served up a pseudo-fingerprint of the city, including St Peter's Basilica in the Vatican. As evening descended amid the murmur of fountains and the clickety-clack of stiletto heels treading on cobblestones, we made our way back to the hotel as the Pantheon, Castel Sant'Angelo and Piazza Navona lit up.

In fairness to Alitalia, they saw to it that we were well fed and watered during our stay in Rome, savouring aperitivos and pasta dinners washed down with fine Italian wines. Much to our relief, on the morning of day four we were told that our flight to Australia was imminent.

Again, we were reminded not to leave the hotel and to have our bags packed and ready for collection at reception. Immediately after breakfast, I went for a short walk around the block. On my return – seemingly out of nowhere - a pack of feral dogs appeared.

My stride soon quickened to a jog, then a sprint. In my haste to outpace the advancing canines, I slipped on some sodden leaves that lay strewn on the footpath. I got back on my feet and fell into the hotel foyer shaken but relieved to end up unscathed, rivulets of sweat running down my face.

The dogs had done me a good turn. And it was highly fortunate that I hadn't dawdled.

Waiting anxiously at reception was an airline rep. We were told to load their luggage on the coach parked alongside the entrance, ready to take us to the airport where our plane to Australia was waiting on the tarmac.

Not all fellow passengers were as fortunate. Some of them couldn't resist the temptation that morning of heading into the city for some last-minute sightseeing. They paid dearly and missed the flight. God only knows how much longer they had to wait to fly Down Under.

On board the plane, I swopped seats with another passenger so I could chat to my new Greek friend, Georgios. He told me that Melbourne was where he and his wife had a restaurant. After Athens, it was the city with the highest number of Greeks anywhere in the world. He asked me to explain to him the reason why I was moving to Australia.

I told him that I was emigrating in the hope of working as a journalist in Perth. I had secured permanent residency and a visa due to a demand for sub editors in Australia. My older brother Liam, who was a doctor and an Australian citizen, had kindly acted as my sponsor.

After watching the movie *Full Metal Jacket*, it was mealtime again. It wasn't long before the soothing effects of the cabernet sauvignon kicked in, and I conked out. On my awakening, Georgios resumed his chatter. He said that when he got to Melbourne, he intended to convert every Australian Rules fan to football – "a proper sport", as he put it. I mentioned that I too liked football and that for my sins I was an Arsenal fan. He replied: "Ahh, Liam Brady! What a player! Irishman too, yeah?"

He gave me a run-down on a 1950 Australian government film, *No Strangers Here*. It told migrants about loving the 'new country' and pressed home the need for them to assimilate into society. Greeks took the message to heart and served up alfresco dining on Melbourne's sidewalks.

Shortly after we took off from Zayed International Airport in Abu Dhabi, Georgios asked me if I knew the background to Australia's most famous tune, 'Waltzing Matilda'. He was met with a blank stare. He said the ballad tells the story of a swagman journeying by foot – 'waltzing'. All his earthy belongings and blankets were stored in a 'matilda', or 'swag', slung over his back.

A swagman, or swaggie, was an itinerant worker. He led a nomadic life, trudging along country roads from farm to farm, looking for seasonal or casual work - a pastime described as being 'on the wallaby'.

At a bush camp beside a billabong, the swagman brews tea in a billy can and grabs a stray 'jumbuck' (sheep) to eat. Soldiers arrive ("up came the troopers, one, two and three") and demand that the swagman surrenders his kill - but he wasn't having any of it.

The word billabong comes from the Wiradjuri Aboriginal community in New South Wales. It describes a pond or pool of water left behind when a river alters course or after floodwaters recede – otherwise known as an oxbow lake.

"Up cut the swagging and jumped into the billabong
'You'll never catch me alive', said he
And his ghost may be heard if you pass by that billabong
Who'll come a Waltzing Matilda with me?"

On the last leg of the flight from Singapore, I decided it was time for another movie, something to distract my mind and 'kill' another couple of hours at least. I watched as Michael Douglas and Glenn Close engaged in a one-night stand that got out of hand in the psychosexual thriller *Fatal Attraction*.

Shortly before the credits rolled, the flight attendant approached our row of seats with breakfast trays. However, having witnessed the infamous bunny boiler scene, I'd no stomach for food, so I politely declined her offer. If only I'd chosen a less gruesome movie to watch, something more cathartic. Robin Williams as a radio DJ in *Good Morning, Vietnam* would have been a wiser call.

Not long to go, and we'd be on the ground again. In Australia, at last. The dawn sky was bright with wispy clouds for company as the plane made its final approach to Sydney International Airport. I peered out the window and revelled at my first sight of the land Down Under.

Below us was the uplifting splendour of Darling Harbor and its crown jewel - the majestic Opera House with its spherical shells shimmering in the distance. It is no exaggeration to describe the building as a masterpiece of human creativity, a valentine to the powers of architecture, construction, and design.

Irishman and structural engineer Peter Rice played a key role in creating the edifice using his mathematical expertise and artistic intuition to convert concrete, steel, and glass into the world-renowned white sails roof.

The opera house took fifteen years to build, and the final cost was fourteen times over budget when work began in 1959. Few people deny it was money well spent. In the run-up to the official opening of the Harbor Bridge in 1932, 60,000 school children were invited to be the first people to make the crossing. Eight-year-old Kenneth Jones climbed to the top of the bridge – without recourse to a harness.

It was time for Georgios and me to say our goodbyes. He was adamant that if ever I was in Melbourne, I must contact him. He handed me his business card. I told him that I'd send on my contact details once I had my accommodation in Fremantle sorted. Despite every good intention, and as happens when like-minded people get acquainted, our paths would never cross again.

A few hours later and I was back on board another plane, this time bound for my final stop - Perth. While my mind flourished with anticipation, little could I envisage the amazing experiences that lay ahead and the unforgettable characters that were about to enter my life.

Chapter 4

Shocking News

"The arc of the moral universe is long, but it bends towards justice" – Martin Luther King

Fremantle, December 1987

The first task I set myself every morning after breakfast was to head to the local newsagent and buy a copy of the *West Australian* newspaper to see if there were any suitable jobs advertised. While most of the content in the *West* comprised reports from around the state and stories of national significance, space was found for major news from overseas.

A few days after Christmas, a news brief from the other side of the world caught my eye. The header read: 'UDA leader assassinated'. The story referred to John McMichael, a senior figure in the Ulster Defence Association (UDA). He was killed instantly as a booby-trap car bomb exploded in the driveway of his home on December 22nd, 1987.

He was about to deliver turkeys to the families of loyalist prisoners. Indoors, his three-year old son, Saul, was playing with a new puppy and was fortunate to avoid injury as part of the car flew into the house. Up to a short time before McMichael's death, he was provided with an around-the-clock bodyguard. He changed his car every fortnight.
In a statement, the Irish Republican Army (IRA) said the attack was a pre-emptive strike against the UDA's Ulster Freedom Fighters (UFF) which planned to bomb Dublin and other towns south of the Border.

Shocking News

McMichael first came to public prominence in the early 1980s when he warned that the IRA hunger strike in Long Kesh would lead to a serious escalation in sectarian violence in the North. He was proved right. It was a time of recurring tit-for-tat murders and bombings which prevailed for another decade.

Six weeks before McMichael's murder, on Sunday, November 8th, 1987, in the town centre of Enniskillen, County Fermanagh, the IRA bombed a Poppy Day remembrance ceremony held in support of the British armed forces.

I recall sitting on my couch in Fremantle, watching the Channel Seven News and hearing about the 40-pound bomb that was left behind the cenotaph at the heart of the parade in Enniskillen.

Eleven people, ten civilians and a Royal Ulster Constabulary (RUC) officer were killed and 63 people injured. The last victim died thirteen years later, having been in a coma since the day of the attack.

Caught up in the explosion that day were Gordon Wilson, a 60-year-old local draper, who was maimed, and his daughter, Marie, a nurse, who was fatally injured by the blast.

I watched in disbelief as Wilson gave an emotional interview to the BBC, just hours after the bombing. He described his last conversation with his daughter as they both lay buried in the rubble, unable to move.

Wilson said that he held his daughter's hand as tightly as he could and comforted her as she lay dying. Her last words before she lost consciousness were: "Daddy, I love you very much." Wilson said: "I bear no ill will. I bear no grudge. Dirty sort of talk is not going to bring her back to life. She was a great wee lassie. She loved her profession. She was a pet. She's dead. She's in heaven and we shall meet again. I will pray for these men tonight, and every night."

Jonathan Bardon, author of *A History of Ulster*, later said that no words in more than twenty-five years of violence in the North had such a powerful and emotional impact. A native of Manorhamilton, Co Leitrim, Wilson later became a peace campaigner and met with leaders of the IRA and their political wing, Sinn Féin. He pleaded with the loyalist paramilitaries that there should be no reprisals.

In 1993, Wilson was nominated by Taoiseach Albert Reynolds as a member of Seanad Éireann. After his death in 1995, Wesley College, the school in Dublin where he attended as a teenager, renamed their library the Gordon Wilson Library in honour of man who wanted to deflect Irish people's vision from the prism of the past. To quote Paul Brady's line from his song 'The Island': "Still trying to carve tomorrow from a tombstone."

Known as 'Big John', McMichael was the deputy commander and leader of the UDA's South Belfast Brigade and a commander of the Ulster Freedom Fighters (UFF), a cover name for the UDA. He was a charismatic character.

His son, Gary, went on to launch the short-lived Ulster Democratic Party, with links to the UDA. He was part of a group that helped broker the loyalist ceasefires in 1994, along with Progressive Unionist Party (PUP) leader David Irvine.

The PUP was aligned with the Ulster Volunteer Force (UVF). It was suspected that the UVF colluded with police officers in the RUC and the British Army's Ulster Defence Regiment (UDR) infantry unit in forming the notorious Glenanne Gang. The group was said to be responsible for 120 killings, including the 1974 Dublin and Monaghan bombings and the 1975 Miami Showband massacre.

The UFF oversaw an assassination campaign against the IRA, targeting prominent republicans in a 'shopping list' sourced from leaked security forces' documents. The IRA claimed responsibility for McMichael's killing.

They said that the attack was carried out by a unit led by Seán Savage, who himself was shot dead along with Mairéad Farrell and Daniel McCann by the British Army's Special Air Service (SAS) on Gibraltar's Winston Churchill Avenue three months later.

However, the RUC and several senior figures in the UDA - not least Andy Tyrie, the group's leader at the time - had grave doubts about the veracity of the IRA statement. They believed that a senior UDA member passed on information to republicans in response to McMichael's threat to put a stop to a racketeering business operating in Belfast at the time.

What prompted me to be surprised by what I read in the *West* that morning was what had happened seventeen years earlier. In 1970, a delegation from Ógra Fianna Fáil (the party's youth wing) in Dún Laoghaire, had met with leaders of the UDA in the party's headquarters on the Newtownards Road in East Belfast.

I was part of the eight-person delegation. John McMichael was one of four senior UDA members with whom we discussed the Troubles in the North for over three hours on that Saturday afternoon.

The talks formed part of the Northern Initiative visits to Belfast and Derry. We organised the trips as part of an effort by young members of 'The Republican Party' - aka the 'Soldiers of Destiny' – to try and do something practical at the height of the Troubles in the North.

The plan was that the initiative would culminate in a major conference in Dublin attended by a cross-section of representatives from political and community groups north and south of the Border.

During our discussions that afternoon, McMichael disclosed that the UDA operated several cells in the Republic. As the meeting was about to end, Tyrie shared a disconcerting thought with us. In truth, his comment bordered on the chilling.

"It's just as well some of our friends in the area don't know that young members of Fianna Fáil are here with us today," he intoned with a small, thin smile. "I'm not sure we could guarantee your safety," he added. Was Tyrie serious, or just bluffing? To this day, I'm none the wiser.

After our group left the UDA offices, we were brought on a tour of East Belfast in a fleet of black taxis run by the loyalist group. We were shown around a social hall where the slot machines provided a source of cash revenue to fund the organisation's activities.

The following day, our group visited the nationalist Ballymurphy estate in West Belfast. We met with community worker Frank Cahill, brother of IRA veteran Joe Cahill, and a man considered to be of the highest standing in his community. Throughout our walking tour, a British Army helicopter hovered overhead.

Cahill assured us that we nothing to worry about. Such aerial surveillance was an everyday occurrence in nationalist estates.

A similar but more worrying incident occurred on our return to the city centre. As our Southern-registered car was driven away from a British Army checkpoint, a Saracen armed personnel carrier followed directly behind us. The soldiers pointed their rifles in plain sight.

Further delegations from Ógra Fianna Fáil Dún Laoghaire later met with prominent public representatives in Belfast, including Social Democratic & Labour Party (SDLP) member John Cushnahan, peace negotiator Father Alec Reid and Robert Bradford, a Methodist minister, and Ulster Unionist Party (UUP) member, who was murdered by the IRA in 1981.

On another visit to Belfast, a delegation went along to one of Ian Paisley's Sunday services at his Martyrs Memorial Free Presbyterian church on the Ravenhill Road. They were invited to sign the visitors book, and everyone wrote down 'Dublin' as their address.

It was a note vague enough for the Democratic Unionist Party (DUP) leader to acknowledge the delegation's presence as "our friends from the Republic". Little did he know that his "friends" were young members of Fianna Fáil. And no harm, either.

My good friend, Declan Flood, was part of the delegation. He said that Paisley delivered a sermon from the pulpit as only he could, followed by a plea for donations. He reminded the congregation of a line from the Bible which implores churchgoers to contribute "a tithe" – a tenth of their personal wealth. When the service ended, the congregation filed out of the church. They queued in the rain to shake Paisley's hand and share a moment.

When word got out in July 1980 about our plans to stage the Northern Initiative conference in Dublin later that year, we were ordered by Fianna Fáil leader and the Taoiseach at the time, Charles J Haughey, to meet with him in his offices the following week.

On our arrival in the hallway of the princely building, we were met by Haughey's private secretary. She escorted us to a room on the first floor. A short time later, he stood by the door, signing documents as fast as they were handed to him.

Impeccably dressed as always, the Taoiseach entered the room, gliding across the deep pile carpet like a hovercraft. He shook each of us by the hand, and we introduced ourselves.

As he stood at one end of the pristine, solid mahogany table, we glanced and smiled gingerly at one another. A moment later, deputy Seamus Brennan entered the room, with a notebook in his hand. He greeted us with a reserved wave, and we all took our seats.

We got straight down to business. Haughey said he had heard a lot about the Northern Initiative. Good or bad? We understood he wasn't too impressed. He wanted to know about our plans for the conference. Specifically, he was keen to learn about our line-up of speakers. We read out a list of names and organisations. Haughey peered at us with his hooded eyes and an irritated sigh.

He paused, before asking us: "Who do you think you are, members of Dún Laoghaire fucking Debating Society?" He said that as leader of Fianna Fáil, he could not possibly stand over its members providing a public platform for individuals or groups that were diametrically opposed to the party.

He expressed firm disquiet at the inclusion of UCC professor and *Sunday Independent* columnist John A Murphy. "Well, you can forget about him," he said, recoiling in his seat, "he's nothing but a bloody Blueshirt!" A short man with a short fuse. Brennan looked up disconcertedly from his notes, his cheeks flushed with embarrassment.

Observing Haughey up close for the first time, it was obvious why he was called 'The Boss'. Despite his diminutive stature, he had an aura about him that soared. He was charismatic, smart, and ruthless. Such traits secured him the approval of his followers, while silencing those who opposed him. With similar cunning, he won over several top Irish businessmen.

It will be left to the history books to interpret Haughey's legacy. While he was reviled and seen as a pariah by his opponents, his supporters hailed him as a national treasure. Regardless of allegiances, he earned recognition for the political changes he orchestrated as a government minister, particularly in the health and justice departments.

Wary in advance that the meeting could spell the end of the Northern Initiative – while, at the same time, fully aware that we were way out of our depth in 'playing politics' - we expressed our hopes for the forthcoming conference and explained how the event could benefit Fianna Fáil.

Haughey was attentive throughout. He insisted that if the conference was to have any chance of proceeding, one thing was certain. "First and foremost," he said, "there will be no invitations extended to anyone from the republican and loyalist paramilitaries."

He said he had no objection to us inviting any of the other speakers on our list, even though it was obvious that they were not the sort of people he would normally willingly entertain. With that, the meeting was over. We stood up in chorus. Haughey shook our hands and left the room.

There was no walk of shame. We departed the Taoiseach's office that day feeling a sense of relief and satisfaction; relief that the conference could now proceed and satisfaction that there were only minor tweaks to our plans.

Full steam ahead!

The conference was staged in Dublin's Mansion House in October 1980. A host of political and community groups from both sides of the Border showed up. The turn-out was encouraging. Journalists covering the event included Frank McDonald and Bruce Arnold. Myles McWeeney broadcast a report with interviews on BBC Radio Ulster.

The House of Commons was represented on the day by Conservative MP Michael Mates who took part in a panel discussion. Mates went on to chair the Northern Ireland Affairs Committee. He was a minister at the Northern Ireland Office from 1992 to 1993. His legacy was tarnished by his support for failed business tycoon Asil Nadir.

As his fellow Conservative MP and highly divisive parliamentary colleague Enoch Powell once famously said: "All political lives, unless they are cut off in midstream at a happy juncture, end in failure - because that's the nature of politics and of human affairs."

Chapter 5

A Move North

"The air feels like a warm bath into which hotter water is trickling constantly" – EM Forster's *Passage to India*

Katherine, March 1988

The need to get out of bed at five o'clock every morning, six days a week to shove junk mail through home letterboxes around Fremantle before the heat got too intense was getting to me. My pay for such menial work barely covered the cost of the bottled water I bought to keep hydrated.

Lazy afternoons were spent on Cottlesloe Beach, but even they grew tiresome. The closure of Robert Holmes à Court's *Western Mail* in Perth meant there were a line of journalists out of work. There are two prime qualifications for getting a job with a newspaper. First, a reasonable ability to write. Second, knowing who's who. While I could get by on the initial requirement, when it came to competing with other job seekers with a well-endowed contact book, the reality was, I hadn't a prayer.

Money was scarce and its fast rate of decrease was matched by a depleting threshold for boredom fast bordering on ennui. Supported by funds provided by Australia's Federal Employment Office, I signed up for a move, to relocate elsewhere. I got an interview for a role as a journalist in the Northern Territory. A few days later, I was informed that if I wanted the job, it was mine.

A Move North

When I told people that I planned to leave Western Australia and move to a remote town in the Top End known for its picturesque gorge and high crime rate, they thought I was either joking or that I had lost my mind. One of them said to me that the only culture anyone is likely to find in Katherine was in a carton of yogurt; a place as far removed from glamorous as it is possible to be.

How could I even contemplate leaving the pristine Perth suburb of Fremantle and its Mediterranean climate to head to Australia's Top End? To a small town like Katherine in the middle of nowhere, where temperatures can soar to 48 degrees Celsius, and humidity reaches punishing levels during the build-up to the wet season.

A mate of mine recalled the time he visited the town. He arrived in the middle of the day. He took a quick look around the place, got something to eat and drink and jumped on the next bus leaving for Darwin. "I couldn't get out of the bloody hellhole quick enough," George cried. "Trust me Mike, you'll hate Katherine."

Oh no, what had I done? I silently asked myself.

The cost of living in Australia's Top End was considerably higher than it was in WA. Foods had to be transported north by road train from places like Adelaide. Energy bills were through the roof. It required keeping the use of air conditioning under control. Clothing was one saving, as the local dress code comprised shorts, singlets, and thongs.

Katherine often seemed airless, skin felt clammy, and your head grew feverish. One weekend afternoon in our house, I was trying to swat an elusive mosquito with a newspaper. The near silent whirr and slow movement of the ceiling fan caught me off guard. The local GP assured me that the gash on my arm didn't require stitches. It took two weeks and a course of antibiotics for it to heal.

In the late 1980s, Katherine, with a population of around 7,000, had the second highest crime rate in Australia *pro rata* after Sydney. It was a landscape suffused with violence and pregnant with suppressed anger. Some people put it down to the Territory's tropical climate, which can meddle with people's mental health.

American travel writer Bill Bryson once remarked that the most striking thing about English or Irish weather was that "there isn't very much of it". For the most part, and certainly when compared to northern Australia, Western Europe has next or no cyclones, monsoons, little humidity – and back then - no major bush fires to worry about.

As climate change takes a firmer hold, and severe floods and drought become the norm, it's hard to know how things will continue to pan out.

In Ireland, there's no real need for air conditioning, you wear the same type of indoor clothing year long, and it's where you don't die from exposure to the elements. Unless, of course, you're the sort of person who's inclined to climb Croagh Patrick in a dressing gown and slippers in February.

A Move North

Luigi Albano, my new boss, was at Darwin Airport to greet me. A diminutive figure with an impish smile, he stood in line at arrivals, holding one of those cards with the names of incoming passengers scrawled in capital letters... MICHAEL CULLEN. Once we recognised one another, he extended a plump hand and a blissful smile. Wet circles seeped out under the arms of his short-sleeved, brown shirt.

Luigi relieved me of my suitcase and insisted on carrying it. As we left the airport terminal and walked towards the carpark, there was no escaping the still and overwhelming heat, moist air, and the bush's pervasive musky odour.

Welcome to the Northern Territory, the Last Frontier! My first St Patrick's Day in Australia.

As we set off on our 315-kilometre, three-hour drive to Katherine, I could sense my life was about to take a dramatic turn. While I absorbed the rusty landscape lying in every direction, my host did the talking. He drew a picture of everyday life in an outback town. He explained what my job at the *Katherine Advertiser* would entail.

Three hours later and Luigi was introducing me to his parents, Gino, and Sofia. The Albano family arrived in Australia from Italy in 1978. They were born and reared in Castelmezzano, a small, provincial town in the mountains of Potenza, in the southern region of Basilicata. They were childhood sweethearts. Castelmezzano was a refuge for bandits in the 19th century because of its many hiding places, something it had in common with Katherine.

Gino thrived on 'hard yakka' and an acceptance of a frugal life. He built the family home from top to bottom and was a dab hand at car repairs. He didn't display taste in anything much, least of all clothes. The black shorts and singlets he wore to work each day masked the accumulations of grime and oil stains.

His command of English was poor, as was his hearing. He chortled, while muttering to himself in Italian. He oversaw collections at Sunday Mass in the local church. Gino's piety, however, never deterred him from telling a joke racy enough to make your teeth blush.

People in Katherine loved and respected the Albanos. They valued Gino's do-it-yourself mentality. He combined teak toughness with congeniality. His property interests provided collateral for a bank loan to buy the newspaper's printing presses.

Luigi ran the business. He was thrifty and a maestro at controlling costs. The newspaper competed for advertising with *The Katherine Times*, part of Rupert Murdoch's ubiquitous News Corp. His two younger siblings, Sandro and Gina, were students. Tattooed on Sandro's arm was a single word in Italian, *osare* - to dare.

The Albano home was mine too, at least until such time as I could find somewhere to rent closer to town. It was warm and welcoming with no indications of familial discord.

Luigi's was devoted to his mother, and it was easy to see why. Sofia was petite and quietly spoken. She stayed on the side of goodness, as did her cooking; every meal she served up a homage to the 'old country'.

Minestrone soup to start. For main course, a dish of spaghetti bolognese so delicious it was not just better than my mother's but perhaps even better than God's. In what appeared to be a drink-sharing ritual at the dinner table, Luigi placed two glasses in front of each diner: one for water, the other for wine. Gino made his way around the table with a jug and poured everyone a measured glass of valpolicella. Refills were not entertained.

Sofia came from a part of Italy where the staple diet was minestra - beans and vegetables from the family's kitchen garden - ingredients not normally associated with Italian cooking. Pasta was only eaten on Sundays and on special occasions. It was served with a modest portion of pork jowl, not the more expensive pork belly.

Meat and fish were considered luxuries. Gino's family ate amatriciana, a tomato-based recipe with bacon, a once a year treat when they could afford to slaughter a pig. Luigi told me there was a myth about carbonara being the food of 18th century Italian charcoal workers. In fact, he said, carbonara was an American dish born in Italy during the Second World War. Up until then, most people in Italy had never heard of it. Pizza took off in southern Italy in the 1940s; it was made and eaten on city streets.

Sofia's dessert was tiramisu. Rejoice! As someone who believes that main courses are simply desserts' appetisers, I'd never tasted such a moreish confection. She told me that it wasn't until the 1980s that tiramisu first appeared in cookbooks. Its star ingredient, mascarpone, was sold only in Milan food stores up until the 1960s. The coffee-infused sponge biscuits that divide the layers are pavesini, a snack first rolled out in 1948.

After a four day-stay at the Albano home, Luigi sorted accommodation for me a stone's throw from the town. Boy-oh-boy, a house on stilts with a veranda and corrugated iron roofs! A few days after the move, I met my new housemate. Phil Shaw, who had travelled up to Katherine from Hobart in Tasmania. He was hired as the newspaper's production manager. We got on famously.

Sharing the house with us was a journalist from Brisbane whom Phil and I worked out right away for who he was. Jonathan Wakeland was adrift in a sea of self-loathing which made it hard for him to get on with people. He was flinty and an officious busybody. Outside of work and our discussions about housekeeping duties, we went our separate ways.

Our accommodation was spartan. Throughout the house there was with an odd vanilla smell which, initially, I blamed on the air conditioning system. Even the sitting room walls, which tracked the geckos' nightly insect raids, exuded the same odour. The translucent lizards were our house guests, cute and self-sustaining little creatures whose dashing forays provided late night entertainment.

Every evening during the build-up, the serenity in our back garden was shattered by a local colony of bats, known as flying foxes. They would flap around at dusk in cauldrons so dense they compounded the darkness. They called to one another as they flew in and out of the tree branches, gorging on ripened mangoes, before returning to their roosts.

So, it came to be myself, Phil, new home, new job, and a whole new world.

Chapter 6

Gentle as a Dove

"The world doesn't need what women have. The world needs what women are" – Edith Stein

Katherine, November 1988

Phil's girlfriend was Helga Breitner, a savvy and exuberant young woman, whose bliss had a halo effect. She defied the oft-held notion that a person of German descent must be precise and a stranger to irony. She had an open heart and a gift of the gab. She could curse like a fishwife, and her throaty rasp made everything she said sound mellifluous.

Helga first arrived in Australia with her family in 1974 at the age of twelve. Like many German immigrants before them, the Breitners settled in South Australia, in the Clare Valley near Adelaide. There they set up a family wine business called 'Grape Expectations'. Her father, Heinrich, cultivated vines from the riesling grape. Helga was raised on the terroir.

She wasn't afraid of hard work and hauling a hod up and down the hill became a doddle to her. The winery's early days were trying, and money was tight. The family lived off the clippings of tin.

Things were so precarious at one point that Heinrich planned to quit and resume his career as a dentist. Chastened by his ill-luck, he refused to be bowed, and his steadfastness paid off. Within a couple of years, the business was profitable.

Helga was a gifted craft-maker. She graduated from art college in Adelaide and trained in jewellery design. She enjoyed dancing – "shakin' her stuff". Her favourite tune was Nena's '99 Red Balloons', which, without any encouragement, she would sing at an astral level – in German.

She liked to paint her nails red. She wore floral dresses with a high hemline, which turned heads. As her partner Phil remarked, cheekily: "Give her a hankie, and she'd wear it!"

Every weekend during the dry season, Helga would jump on her motorbike and head off to the bush. It was her cathedral, where she went to play with nature. She was unmindful of the risks in travelling off-road on two wheels at speed, even with brakes that demanded a degree of forward planning. Not to mention trying to ditch potholes the size of an Olympic pool.

She set great store in scrambling across the red earth and navigating stretches of rock desert and loose gravel. On her return trip home, she would stop off at Katherine hot springs and take a dip in the thermal baths to soothe the aches caused by hours in the saddle. When riding her bike, Helga felt exhilarated. The sense of empowerment allowed her mind run on empty, her body bubbling with adrenalin. "When I'm out there on my Suzuki, I think of nothing at all - it's pure meditation - freedom," Helga told me. She loved how Robert M Pirsig captured the thrill of riding a bike in his book, *Zen and the Art of Motorcycle Maintenance*: "... you're completely in contact with it all, you're in the scene and not just watching it anymore, and the sense of presence is overwhelming."

Helga's life had not always been a coaster ride. Adolescent experiences seared in her memory unmoored her. At the age of 14, in the wake of a close friend's death, she developed a dysfunctional relationship with food.

She had a phobia about gaining weight and body-image disturbance. Her emaciated condition led to concerns about her physical, mental, and emotional health.

She convinced herself that eating normally was a sign of personal weakness. When her weight dropped to less than six stone, Helga had to be hospitalised and force-fed. Her doctors warned her parents that their daughter was not only at risk from malnutrition, but there was also a danger she might self-harm.

For people with anorexia, the prefrontal cortex, which combines personal values and social expectations, is thought to have too much power. Women are more vulnerable to the disease as they strive for perfection in a patriarchal society where they are sexualised and judged by their bodies. Helga underwent psychiatric therapy and was put on a nutritional programme to help her regain weight.

After 18 months, she had won the lottery of survival, but it took her almost four years to get to grips with her mental anguish. Medical experts believe that less than one in three people in similar circumstances are as fortunate.

She saw an opportunity and was intent on living her life with passionate advocacy. She channelled her energies into nurturing oxytocin - the hormone of love.

Helga was no Pollyanna and accepted that the world was not all sweetness and light. She eschewed perfectionism, liking it to a mirage. "Let's face it, most people are mediocre," she said. "We get psyched up and strive to be top dog. We should accept average and allow life's messiness sort itself out. Be yourself to the nth degree. Be authentic. You've got to put up with a shower if you want a rainbow."

Shortly after her move to Katherine in 1987, Helga got a job at the local Elders cattle station supplies store. She enjoyed working and was fastidious about her duties. Customers thought the world of her for her moxie – her boldness. She spoke enthusiastically to all-comers and scored on verbal swordplay. She talked to farmers about the trials of delivering a new-born calf and would gladly recommend the best sheep drench.

It was while she was at work one day that Helga met Phil for the first time. From that moment on, it was a story of blossoming love. After furtive glances and halting advances, they were soon spending time together, day and night. He was seduced by her artistry in turning up the volume in his life.

Each day, without fail, Helga called to the house after work to see Phil. They would fire up the barbie, crack open a few tinnies and spend hours chatting and joking under the canopy of the stars. The couple were smitten, lustful and beyond shame when it came to the wiles of the bedroom.

Gentle as a Dove

She quoted lines from the *Kama Sutra*, Vatsyayana's Hindu text on sexuality, eroticism, and emotional fulfilment in life from around the third century. She saw it as a guide on how to live well and explore natural intimacy.

Phil and Helga's romance took off like a comet. Their appetite for lovemaking was robust, in contrast with our house and its wafer-thin walls. The pounding provoked shocks in me that the wooden foundations were at greater risk than they were during the tree-bending electric storms that struck late at night during the build-up.

An incident at a friend's house party caught everyone off-guard. At some point late in the night, Helga and Phil decided it was time they were alone and close, so they slipped outside. In the back garden was a mobile home. They could see from the moonlight that the door was left slightly open. They entered, cautiously.

The caravan was old and rusty, a space unfit for a young, energetic pairing. The bed was so cramped it could have been designed for a hobbit. Minutes later... Bang! The chassis collapsed and the body of the caravan crashed to the ground with a thump. Shaken but unharmed, the libidinous couple scrambled from the vehicle on all fours, rumbling with laughter.

Several partygoers heard the shrieks and went outside to investigate. The incident was a topic of conversation in Katherine over the coming days. Small town, fast gossip. The stories were freighted with their own drama. The event became the couple's legend. Phil saw to it that not so much as a word about the tryst appeared in print.

Chapter 7

Somewhere to Hide

"Power is when we have every justification to kill, and we don't" – Thomas Keneally

Katherine, April 1988

Sleepy outback towns like Katherine act as convenient hideaways for people on the run or those who simply don't wish to be found. Fugitives flee from cities on the east coast and other populated parts of Australia and move to the Top End where they lie low for a period. To mask their identity, some runaways adopt a fictitious name and become great pretenders.

It is estimated that as many as 38,000 people in Australia disappear, or stray, every year – that's a missing person every three hours. Some of them lose their way in the bush, get disoriented by the heat, or find themselves blinded by the vast darkness, and are never seen again.

Chris Burton was the caretaker and swim coach at the Katherine Aquatic Centre operated by the local council. He arrived five years earlier from Queensland, from a town called Bundaberg which gave its name to the dark rum better known as Bundy.

He was a ringer for one of Australia's most well-known celebrities - Paul Hogan, the actor with the sun-bleached hair and cork hat who played the title role in the hit comedy *Crocodile Dundee*. Hogan also famously fronted global advertising campaigns for Foster's lager with the line: 'G'day from the Golden Throat Charmer'.

Chris and I got on well. When it came to local gossip, he was a fount of knowledge. The problem was, he tended to rub people up the wrong way. He was prone to mood swings; one day he might be vivacious and outgoing, the next tetchy and high-handed.

"Mike, did you hear about our drama?" he said. "Crikey, it was pandemonium here the other day. A woman collapsed by the pool. I'd say she was about thirty... looked strong and fit. An ambulance was on the scene in no time. She suffered heat exhaustion after losing body heat through sweat."

Chris was a qualified paramedic. He said that when a person's temperature touches 40 degrees, they suffer heatstroke. Blood gets diverted from key organs. It can result in permanent brain damage - or death. The normal body temperature is 37 degrees; the skin is cooler at 33 to 35 degrees. To avoid excessive temperatures, blood transfers heat to the skin, where it diffuses.

When the air is hotter than the skin, a person remains cool by producing sweat, which takes heat away as it evaporates. Humans can sweat up to 20 litres a day, each litre consumes 580 calories of energy while the air is dry. When humidity is low, sweating works. But when high temperatures and moistened air combine, the body can't keep losing heat through sweat.

The woman was taken to Katherine Hospital. She was kept in for tests. Nothing showed up and the doctors decided to discharge her the next day. "She was back here yesterday, not a bother on her, doing laps," Chris said. "We'd a good chinwag. She remembered everything about the incident."

She told Chris that when she collapsed, her whole body felt as if it was made from thin, brittle glass. "I'll tell you one thing kiddo; I reckon she was one lucky sheila," he remarked with gusto.

The woman was from Mataranka, about an hour's drive south of Katherine. The small town earned worldwide fame following the success of Jeannie Gunn's autobiography *We of the Never Never* (1908), which was set on the nearby one million-acre Elsey cattle station. In 1982, the book was adapted and became an award-winning film of the same name, and starred Angela Punch McGregor.

Local cops and journalists could rely on Chris for tip-offs. He was happy to point out any "mongrels" who visited the centre, intruders who used the camouflage of the bush and the anonymity of a town like Katherine to go unnoticed. Some were grifters; others had a history of violence. Not exactly your Ned Kelly bushranger, but a possible law and order threat, nonetheless.

Chris told me about an incident which took place shortly after he arrived in Katherine in 1985. The police issued an all-points bulletin (APB) following an incident in a bottle shop in Tennant Creek, an eight-hour drive from Katherine.

A female checkout attendant was bludgeoned by a man with a heavy weapon thought to be a claw hammer. Her injuries were serious but not life-threatening. The cops in Katherine issued a full description of the attacker. Shops had posters with his photo, warning members of the public that the man was armed and dangerous – and that under no circumstances should they consider confronting him.

The next day, a woman called to the police station. She reported seeing "an odd-looking bloke" loitering at the far end of town. The man was in his middle to late forties, about six foot tall, unkempt, and of stocky build. He wore a black tee-shirt emblazoned with an image of the rock band Midnight Oil, a grey cap, and sunglasses – all common enough attire in the outback. She said he was heading in the direction of the aquatic centre. He moved with an awkward gait.

Detective Shane Clarke had a clipped manner and a reputation for being as spiky as a bag of porcupines. He boasted an ego visible from space. That said, he was respected by his peers for being "comprehensive in his efficiency" in apprehending criminals. Clarke phoned Chris to ask him if he had noticed anyone from out of town in the centre that day who may have been acting suspiciously.

"Now that you mention it," Chris said, "there was a chap who showed up at reception around lunchtime. When I asked if I could be of any help to him, he blanked me, which I thought was a bit sus. He then headed out to the pool." Clarke described the suspect's appearance and mentioned that he walked with a slight limp, as if nursing a dodgy hip.

He asked Chris to take a moment and look outside to see if the suspect might still be around. As it happened, he spotted the man sitting in the shade, watching swimmers doing laps of the pool. "Good on ya mate!" Clarke said, excitedly. "We're on our way over right now. Don't take your eyes off the bloody scoundrel... okay!"

A short time later, Clarke and two uniformed coppers arrived at the centre. Chris met them at reception. They told him the plan of action. The cops then went outside and approached the suspect as he sat on a sun lounger. They had a brief chat after which the man was instructed to accompany them to reception.

Inside the centre, the suspect was asked to confirm his name and address. He refused to say what the reason was for him being in Katherine that day. Clarke and his sidekick tried a 'good-cop, bad-cop' tactic, but the man was defiant. He had no intention of helping them with their investigations.

Clarke read him his rights. As he placed him in handcuffs, he noticed that the palms of his hands were excoriated by an act of hard labour. While being shown into the back of the paddy wagon, he studied Chris with a stare that radiated malice. He stabbed the air with his hand.

The interview resumed at Katherine police station. The suspect demanded legal aid and refused to answer questions until his lawyer arrived. An exasperated Clarke warned him not to take him for a fool: "Bloody oath... don't come the raw prawn with me."

The detainee's lawyer convinced him that it was in his best interest to co-operate and answer the questions the police put to him. Despite denying all the accusations, he was charged with violent assault and threatening behaviour. He was remanded in custody overnight.

The next morning, the interrogation resumed, with his solicitor again present. The sleepover paid off as the suspect was more compliant – or so it appeared, at first. He gave his name as Larry Thompson. He was then brought before a special hearing of the magistrates' court.

The cops were convinced that the man was lying about his identity, that he was not who he said he was, and that Thompson was an alias he had adopted. They believed that the incident in Tennant Creek was one of a string of violent crimes he had committed in recent years.

Their gut feelings about his mendacity were correct. They confirmed the man's identity from fingerprint records. He was one Jock Rogers, a 43-year-old unemployed engineer with an address in Darwin. He was known to police.

Tall and well-built with a lantern face and a pudding bowl haircut, his years of peripatetic living and bad decisions had done him no favours. His mien resembled the lead protagonist in *Suttree*, Cormac McCarthy's powerful semi-autobiography about drunks and scoundrels in Knoxville, Tennessee in the 1950's.

He was shunned in his local community. A warrant for his arrest was issued after a series of attacks on women. He was a devout preyer. Social services records indicated that he had a history of coercive control over his former partner.

In 1985, the woman vanished without trace.

Rogers' ex was a type one diabetic. The cops suspected that he may have given her a lethal injection of insulin after they found half-empty vials beneath a bedroom cabinet. It made no sense for the woman to hide her medication. An insulin overdose can - if not counteracted in time with an infusion of glucose or carbohydrate - result in the victim becoming comatose or dying.

With his guile in avoiding arrest, police dubbed Rogers 'The Chameleon'. When cops called to his home, they found the doors of the derelict house padlocked and the windows boarded. They used a ram to force entry. A sweep of the property uncovered a Winchester rifle, two handguns, a cache of ammunition, and hunting knives, all stored in the attic.

Sulphuric acid, sedatives, a bow saw, and hanks of rope were stashed in kitchen cupboards. The homicide unit extended the search to a garden shed. There, cadaver dogs unearthed sealed plastic bags with blood-stained clothes. Wooden planks concealed a shallow grave with partly decomposed human remains from which slivers of flesh were shaved off. The stench of putrefaction was overpowering.

Clarke said it was hard to fathom how anyone could stoop so low in their disregard for fellow humans. Rogers underwent psychiatric tests. He was diagnosed as being unhinged and psychopathic. The crime team felt they had ample evidence to convict him of murder. To complete the macabre jigsaw, the cops sought a prime witness.

A week later, the cops interviewed Rogers' next-door neighbour. The man was retired and lived alone. In a statement, he said he was outside in his back garden one night having a smoke, when he heard a noise, the ruffle of someone digging in the next garden. He peeked through an opening in the fence. A light beam from a spotlight extended along the ground allowed him to catch a glimpse of a tall, well-built man emerging from the shed with a shovel. He recognised him as his neighbour.

The witness statement was crucial in the prosecution's testimony. Police reported that ballistic and forensic tests connected Rogers to two murders – one male, the other female. Dental records and an absence of an insulin overdose from the postmortem examination proved that the female victim was not Rogers' constant companion – what Aussies refer to as a *de facto*. She remained a missing person and the case was unresolved.

On the first day of a four-week trial in Darwin Supreme Court, Rogers' lawyer entered a defence of automatism. He told the court that his client was mentally unstable at the time the crimes were committed, and that he could not be held criminally responsible for his actions. The judge regarded the argument as seditious. He ordered the jury to ignore it and the trial should proceed as before.

All nine jurors found the accused guilty on two counts of first-degree murder and a single charge of aggravated assault – namely the shop incident in Tennant Creek. Rogers held to his non-guilty plea. He showed no remorse for his victims. The judge sentenced him to a minimum of 22 years in jail, with no consideration for parole.

The murders evoked an echo of the barbarism in Seamus Heaney's lyrical translation of the epic Old English poem *Beowolf*. The protagonist, Grendel, was a creature of darkness who lurked and swooped on his prey. Heaney described him as "the terror-monger" and "captain of evil", who in waging his lonely war inflicted "atrocious hurt".

Four months after the court case concluded, Clarke was promoted to chief superintendent. Despite his unyielding demeanour and vaulting ambition, it was seen by his fellow officers as a just reward for his competence in tackling crime over many years in the Northern Territory.

A cop in Katherine said to me: "Mike, funny thing is, Clarkey may not be the sharpest tool in the box. Some folks would say he couldn't organise a bucket of sand in the desert - but he's a fixer. You know what I mean."

Chapter 8

Living the Laugh

"Arts and culture aren't the cherry on the cake, they are the cake" – Melvyn Bragg

Katherine, June 1988

When Irish singer and comedian Geraldine Doyle took to the stage, she told the audience that she had a nickname for her husband Paddy Fitzpatrick. She called him Horizontal. "The only time he's vertical," Ger said, "is when he's at the bar." Australia warmly embraced the pint-sized, curly-haired entertainer from Ireland.

She was in Katherine as part of a sold-out, nationwide tour. A regular guest on Ray Martin's midday shows on the Nine Network, she could see humour in anything, and her hilarity was a balm. On labour pains: "It's like getting your bottom lip and slowly stretching it over the top of your head – it never goes back either."

Reared in Dublin's Herbert Place, near Baggot Street Bridge, one of her brothers was the famous folk singer, Danny Doyle, whose songs included 'Whiskey on a Sunday' and 'A Daisy a Day'. She was one of a family of ten. "We were so poor we had to ambush Meals-on-Wheels," she quipped.

Throughout her show, she tells jokes which deflate the Aussie male ego, a daring exercise in a country renowned the world over as a bastion of male chauvinism. "How come you never tell me when you've had an orgasm?" Bruce asked his partner. To which she replied: "Because you're never there."

When Ger emigrated to Australia in 1972, she and Paddy settled in Sydney. She made guest appearances on the Nine Network's daytime show hosted by the garrulous Mike Walsh. She told the show's producers that she was a singer, not a comic.

When they heard stories about her family ("My mam once told me men are like seagulls. It doesn't pay to look up to them") and what it was like growing up in Ireland, they suggested that she should turn to comedy. It was then that Paddy gave up his career in computers. He became Ger's manager, lighting man and occasional drummer – and a willing target for her gags.

"We have just the one kid. (Son Conor is an actor). Only for those Horizontal tosses and turns in his sleep, we would never have had him. I just caught him on a roll one night. Horizontal – God, he can drink!" she'd say. "He'd climb over ten naked women to get to a bottle of beer. It takes him a while, mind you."

Apart from interludes with comic songs, her repertoire of one-liners came fast and furious. "On my honeymoon, I felt like Scottie out of *Star Trek*," she said. "When I saw Horizontal in the nude I rushed over to the window, looked up into the sky and said: 'Captain, it's like nothing I've seen before. There's absolutely no sign of intelligent life. For God's sake Scottie, beam him up.'"

She told jokes about religion which she may well have had to refrain from sharing with a more God-fearing audience in Ireland. "I'm a retired Catholic," she said. "If I went to confession, I'd have to bring a packed lunch."

Living the Laugh

Ger recalled her convent days. Sister Septicemia asked her had she ever entertained impure thoughts. "No," she assured the nun, "they entertained me."

She once guested at a corporate breakfast. The event organiser informed her he was about to introduce her, before going out on stage and announcing: "Ladies and gentlemen, it's the moment you've all being waiting for. I know, I can't quite believe our luck. We've spared no expense in getting the main event here, arriving earlier by chauffeur-driven car. Yes, that's right, no expense was spared. So, here they are… your prawns! Oh, and Geraldine Doyle is going to do some comedy."

Observing a moment of solemnity for a change, Ger grudgingly admitted that being a female performer had its challenges. She believed that men were more withering and felt threatened by women stand-ups. When a man walks on stage, the audience presumes he's funny. When a woman steps out, she must prove that she can tell a joke.

Is nothing sacred on stage, beyond ridicule? There were two subjects she regarded as taboo, of which she didn't make light. "There's nothing amusing about rape, and Irish jokes are racist and hurtful," she concluded. Every Irish gag in her show was told with affection. What she missed most about Ireland was the craic – "you can't beat it, can you?"

As for her wider world, nothing compared to a laugh: she lived for that.

Chapter 9

Hunter Gatherer

"Forget your perfect offering. There is a crack in everything. That's how the light gets in" – 'Anthem' by Leonard Cohen

Katherine, December 1988

During my time living in Katherine, I got acquainted with an Aboriginal man by the name of Kuparr Barambah. His father, Noah, was a member of the Kalkarindji Aboriginal community that staged a historic work strike in 1966. The Wave Hill walk-off followed years of exploitation, violence, and murders of local Aboriginals.

Wave Hill lies 500 kilometres south of Katherine in the Victoria River district of the Northern Territory. In a stand against meagre food, tobacco, and clothing rations in return for hard work, stockman Vincent Lingiari led 200 people off the eponymous cattle station. The dispute lasted seven years.

Noah Barambah was among the striking stockmen that moved to Wattie Creek, Aboriginal land within Wave Hill's boundaries, where they proposed to set up their own co-operative. The local cattle station was owned by Vesteys, a Darwin-based, family-run meat company.

It was not until 1975 that communities living in the Gurindji region finally got justice. Noah attended a ceremony at Wattie Creek as Australia's prime minister Gough Whitlam returned the land to its traditional owners by pouring red earth into Lingiari's cupped hand.

Hunter Gatherer

The Vesteys kept a low profile but the walk-out at Wave Hill catapulted them into the spotlight as it became the birthplace of the Aboriginal land rights movement. Lingiari was quoted as saying: "I bin thinkin' this bin Gurindji country. We bin here longa time before them Vestey mob."

Kuparr was just a 'boorie', a young boy, at the time of the strike in 1966. His father told him that the Vesteys did nothing to support the local people in return for the backbreaking work and atrocious conditions they were obliged to endure. "They used them, just like slaves," Kuparr said. "They didn't like us (Aboriginals)."

In stark contrast to the persecution and hardship experienced by Indigenous Australians, an air of romance and intrigue surrounds the Aboriginals love of bush food, known as bush tucker. It is down to the symbiotic relationship they have had for 60,000 or more years in foraging for native flora and fauna.

Today, there are about 6,500 identified species of native edibles with nutritional and medicinal powers. Kuparr was delighted to share with me all he knew about bush tucker and Aboriginal traditions.

Kuparr ('red earth') lived off the land at Wattie Creek since he was a teenager. His family's staple diet comprised wichetty grub, berries, freshwater mussels, and barramundi. Wichetty grub is the most widely known bush food eaten by Aboriginal people. The grub is a fleshy, white, wood-eating larvae of the ghost moth which feeds on the roots of the wichetty bush.

The grub is found in the deserts of the outback and is still considered an essential part of the Aboriginal diet. Grub meat is highly nutritious and rich in protein. It is normally eaten live and raw, but some people cook it on a fire or barbecue and serve it as an appetiser. Its flavour can best be described as a cross between chicken and prawn meat; some people say it tastes like scrambled egg.

Kuparr told me that the freshwater mussels (gurruk) bury themselves in the mudbanks of drying creeks. Anyone fishing for them should look out for little holes along the mud banks where they can pull the mussels out. He was partial to lemon myrtle, used in sweet dishes like shortbread and cheesecake, and on savoury pastas, baked fish, and lamb chops.

Other treats included finger limes, gumbi gumbi (native apricot), bush tomato (desert raisin) and the Kakadu plum (gubinge or billygoat plum), which is packed with antioxidants. Green in colour, the plum is said to be the fruit with the highest level of vitamin C in the world.

Emus have a liking for quandong. After eating their fill of the wild peach, they spread the seeds in their excrement. From emu poo springs the next generation of quandong trees. In recent years, the fruit has been in decline in the Northern Territory due to the impact of feral camels – whose numbers have soared - and the plant has been listed as vulnerable. There are now one million wild camels in Australia and the population my double in size every nine years. Across the Territory, camels roam across 40 per cent of the land area.

The Aboriginals have their own methods of removing toxins from foods. They invented what is called the bicornual basket, which serves as a purifying sieve. By placing the basket in running water loaded with ground seeds, the toxins leach out.

During the build-up to the wet season, large amounts of wild berries grow on small trees and shrubs beside freshwater streams. Once the berries turn black, they are ripe and ready to harvest. Kuparr boiled the fruit in a big round black pot. Like a witch's brew, it magically transformed into a vibrant purple extract which is used in the making of women's baskets.

Flower stems of water lilies are hollow and juicy. For me, they tasted a lot like celery sticks. The root tuber has edible seeds which are dug up in the dry season. The starchy seeds are ground into a paste used in cake-making. The cakes are wrapped in lily leaves and paper bark before being baked in a ground oven called a gungerri.

Wattle tree seeds have been a staple for Aboriginals for at least 4,000 years. The highly nutritious seeds are stacked with protein, iron, and fibre. Eaten dried or green, they are roasted or ground into flour for bread. As well as been a superfood, the nitrogen in wattles acts a natural fertiliser, regenerating poor quality soil and preventing erosion. The nitrogen produces grasses which create a new ecosystem for small animals and plants.

Saltbush, which extracts salt from the soil, is fire-retardant and is planted to protect the drought-resistent wattles from bush fires. Farmers use it as sheep feed which improves the quality, flavour, and texture of the meat, and drives up the stock's value.

Kuparr explained to me the workings of the didgeridoo and how Aboriginals used the musical instrument for centuries to teach and pass on stories. He told me that the 'didj' was still played at cultural ceremonies. Originally, it was made from wood taken from trees hollowed by termites.

The didj is a must at corroborees, sacred ceremonies where communities engage with the Dreamtime through creative interactions with music, costume, and dance. A corroboree is sacred to Aboriginal people and only locals are allowed to take part or observe.

A person can stand, sit in a chair, or lie on the ground while playing a didj. A calm mindset is what's important, Kupaar said. Playing a didj is down to lip vibrations and breathing techniques.

When mastered, didj playing is said to help strengthen lung capacity and reduce the effects of asthma and sleep apnea. One old myth was that if an Aboriginal woman was to play the didj - or even touch the instrument - she immediately became pregnant.

The art of body painting has deep spiritual significance in Aboriginal culture. Decorations include face and torso designs used in rituals and the transformation of a figure to form living images of ancestral creatures.

Scarring was mainly used as part of ceremonies to mark age, initiation or to raise a person's status. Body painting is not necessarily just about visual artistic creativity, it relates to rituals, laws, and religion.

As the wet season ended, I headed out to the outskirts of town and meet Kuparr at dusk. "How's it goin' bunji (mate)?" he'd always say. We'd watch small brush fires being lit under controlled conditions. Rather than the coloniser's perception of fire as a destructive force, Aboriginals have used it to manage the land; and the earth is sacred.

Fire is intrinsic to Aboriginal culture. Gum tree leaves are burnt to create the scent of Mother Earth through smoke, which helps ward off evil spirits. Aboriginals recognise fire as a creature that needs to be tamed. For many centuries, they use cool burning, a practice with symbolic meaning.

Fires are lit to clear the underbrush, creating habitats for small animals. Cool burning helps prevent lightning and wildfires from consuming flora and fauna. It rejuvenates the vegetation and preserves the tree canopy. After dark and around dawn are the best times for fires. Nightly dew helps cool down the blaze. Low fires are lit in small areas on foot, using matches or sticks.

The blazes are closely monitored, ensuring that only the underbrush is burnt. Cool burns clear the land and ensures that seeds and nutrients in the soil are not baked and destroyed. Care is taken so as not to increase rainfall runoff. The runoffs deposit soil particles in streams and lakes, cause pollution and reduce local water quality.

Eucalyptus trees suck up water and burn fast. Aboriginals know of at least three species of birds that spread fire. They do so by picking up smouldering sticks, taking them to other grassy areas as a way of flushing potential prey. Scientists say that as the effects of climate change accelerate, so too will the impact of bush fires on communities.

In parts of Australia, all-out fire bans are in place. That means no solid-fuel barbecues or campfires, but also no angle-grinders or welding in the open. The taking of four-wheel drive vehicles off-road is banned, and even electric fences are prohibited.

The work done by firefighters in rural parts of Australia is entirely voluntary. It is like the selfless service the Royal National Lifeboat Institution (RNLI) provides along the coasts of Britain and Ireland. People living near bushland or grassland are at most risk, but random burning of leaves and bark can easily carry fires forward on the wind.

Nowadays, public warnings are issued by local authorities throughout Australia on what steps should be taken to protect lives and homes, such as clearing leaves and debris from their properties. People are ordered to protect their homes with hoses and a proper water supply.

Should a fire approach a residential area, people must close windows, doors, and vents, fill baths, sinks and buckets with water, turn off gas, wet outdoor surfaces facing the fire and check for spot fires. With climate change and global warming, wildfires are not going away. Quite the contrary, the threat continues to escalate.

Over the course of my friendship with Kuparr, I learned about the importance of walkabout in Aboriginal culture. The practice is seen as a rite of passage when young men leave home to experience a journey during their adolescent years, any time between the age of ten to sixteen. The young men live in the wilderness for a period of up to six months as they make the spiritual and traditional transition into manhood.

The wider world got a wonderful insight into the meaning of walkabout from a 1971 film of the same name. *Walkabout* tells the story of two white schoolchildren from a high-rise apartment in Sydney. The youngsters are abandoned by their father in the outback in cruel circumstances and must fend for themselves.

Directed by Nicolas Roeg and based on the novel by James Vance Marshall, the film stars English actress Jenny Agutter, who shot to fame after playing a lead role in the 1970 film version of *The Railway Children*.

David Gulipil plays Black Boy, who helps the young city dwellers survive in the bush. In 2005, the British Film Institute included *Walkabout* in its list of the fifty films everyone should see by the age of fourteen. Kuparr told me that despite everything, he was a proud Australian and he loved his country - a land of ancient cultures which had transformed into a multi-ethnic melting pot.

Chapter 10

Plagued by Violence

"Murder is always a mistake. One should never do anything that one cannot talk about after dinner" – Oscar Wilde

Katherine, February 1989

My work in the Northern Territory was never dull or tiresome – quite the opposite. I was assigned to report on hearings at Katherine Magistrates Court two or three days a week. The experience was an eye-opener. The criminal cases normally centred on acts of domestic violence, from harassment and sexual assault to manslaughter and murder charges.

Walking along Katherine's main street day or night was a touch uncomfortable. It was not unusual to see men and women whose lives were ruptured by misfortune. While passers-by were seldom under threat, it created a frisson of unease, which in the hours of darkness extended to a niggling fear, particularly in the isolated parts of town.

In readiness for writing up my first court reports, I was determined to learn what the most appropriate term was when referencing Indigenous Australians. Was it acceptable to use the word 'tribe'? In the Aboriginal context, a tribe is a group of people related by genealogy, language and living in a recognised area of land. However, it's a European word with colonial connotations. So, I thought it might be best to give that one a miss.

Plagued by Violence

Was the word 'clan' appropriate? A clan is larger than a family but is based on ties through ancestry and language. A high percentage of Aboriginals regard the word 'nation' as acceptable to describe people who share the same language and land. It explains the use of the term First Nations' people.

It seemed odd to me that the word Indigenous Australians favour most in identifying themselves is 'mob'. It's not deemed offensive to ask an Aboriginal the question, "to which mob do you belong?" Despite that, the description I believed was the most appropriate to use was 'community'.

Many of the criminal cases that came before the court in Katherine related to domestic violence. What may start out as a quarrel could get out of hand, with tragic results. The violence was often fuelled by alcohol – the dreaded "grog".

One Aboriginal woman came before the magistrate charged with violent behaviour. She was accused of beating her partner senseless and slashing his face with a kitchen knife. On seeing the woman sober before the magistrate, it was hard to imagine her capable of such a terrible act. She demanded that "her man" take her fishing, but he had other plans.

The legal blood alcohol content (BAC) for a fully licensed driver is 0.05 of alcohol per 100 millilitres of blood. It was not unusual for someone to appear in court on drink-driving charges who were two, three and four times over the legal limit. Less frequently, arrests were made where the person was a staggering five or six times over the limit.

The Northern Territory's pathologist, Dr Kevin Lee, carried out blood-alcohol tests in all postmortem examinations as a matter of routine, regardless of age. To the best of Dr Lee's knowledge - and he worked all over the world - it was a medical practice unique to the Territory. Levels of alcohol were even found in suckling babies.

In another case, a young father was in court to hear State evidence on the death of his ten-week-old child. Dr Lee's postmortem examination revealed the infant had 15 broken ribs and a fractured skull. The baby's parents, aged 19 and 21, had a history of drug abuse.

The preliminary hearings in murder trials were held in Katherine Magistrates Court before being transferred to the Supreme Court in Darwin for a full sitting. Some cases involved minors and were held in-camera, which meant that the media could not report on the proceedings.

One murder case stood out for me. Both defence and prosecution counsel referred to a long list of details from a pathology report presented at the victim's inquest. The crime was something you might expect to see in the bloodiest revenge or horror movie. It happened in an Aboriginal community less than eight kilometres from Katherine.

My editor instructed me to note down every word said in court that morning. By the time the proceedings ended, the deadline for the newspaper's midweek edition was less than two hours away. As soon as I arrived back to the office, I shared the story with my editor. He told me to type up my report as soon as possible.

Plagued by Violence

The editor decided to lead the front page with a headline, which read: 'Local man on murder charge'. Brief background details on the victim and the accused man appeared in the first two paragraphs. At the time of the murder, he was living just outside Katherine and was a member of a wider Aboriginal community in the Top End. However, by the time the edition went to press, the headline that ran was more shocking.

It was five-thirty on a Friday evening, time for a beer.

In fact, it was no different to any other end of week in Katherine. With just a skeleton crew required to work at the *Advertiser* at weekends, most of my colleagues at the newspaper knocked off early and met for drinks at the town's Back Bar. It would not be wrong to describe the pub's regular patrons as a motley crew who luxuriated in boisterous revelry.

The bar was packed - and the fun was just starting. At about nine o'clock, Kathy, who worked in advertising sales at the newspaper, invited everyone back to her house, which was about a ten-minute walk from the pub. Members of the local skydiving club joined us. Shiny, happy daredevils, with a penchant for smoking weed. Everyone seemed to be in top firm. An impromptu party was soon in full swing.

Someone played guitar and sang the 'Sound of Silence'. A feisty rendition of 'Waltzing Matilda' followed - the perfect cue for a singalong. Others shuffled together on bean bags and began playing cards. In attendance that night was a colourful colleague of mine by the name of Ray Nichols.

Ray was a beguiling character, a lovable rogue with untamed charisma – what Aussies call a larrikin. He had ink-black eyebrows, scuzzy dreadlocks, and a beard covering his chiselled jawline. All he needed was a bandana and he could have doubled for Johnny Depp as the swashbuckling Captain Jack Sparrow in *Pirates of the Caribbean*.

He wrote for fun. That's how he saw it.

If the editor was to ask him for an article on why it was that only koalas eat eucalyptus leaves, his response would be: "No worries boss, how many words... what's the deadline?" For good measure, he'd offer to organise pics of the "lucky little bastards" who get to sleep for nineteen hours a day.

Ray was happiest when skydiving, seeing nothing but invitation in its power. The rebel in him didn't subscribe to mortal dangers; he exuded an air of invincibility. The tattoo inked on his neck described the highs he felt every time he jumped out of a light aeroplane at 10,000 feet. The inscription read: "Falling with grace, soaring with freedom."

Ray's head for heights was in his DNA.

He told me that his grand-uncle Bill was a tightrope walker. He performed in the same circus troupe as Australian legend Con Colleano. In 1936, Colleano became the first person to successfully attempt a forward somersault on a high wire. He became a famous name in world sport. Adolf Hitler is said to have offered the 'Wizard of the Wire' a German passport.

Skydiving wasn't for me. There were too many mad stories about accidents where people fell to their deaths or were left paralysed. My thoughts were fixed on what could happen if the parachute failed. Ray told me I was a scaredy-cat. He pointed to the reserve parachute as a safeguard.

But what if I'd jump out of the plane into the air and the second chute refused to open? Or the chute lines got tangled? Ray was adamant that accidents seldom occur. Or, as he so delicately put it, while smashing a beer can on his forehead, "they're as rare as rocking horse shit".

Statistics showed that for every 1,000 skydives undertaken, only one ends in serious injury or death. Problem was, I lived in terror of being that stat. It was up there in the big fears' stakes, along with having my fortune told. "Why worry, mate," Ray said with trademark abandon, "life is short. After that, we're all compost."

Ray and I both loved to laugh. We were huge fans of Tommy Cooper. So, we began telling jokes. Ray went first. "Saw my mate outside the doctor's today, looking worried. 'What's the matter?' I asked. 'I've got the big C,' he said. 'What, cancer?' 'No, dyslexia'." My turn. "A guy walks into the psychiatrist wearing only clingfilm for shorts. The shrink says, 'Well, I can clearly see you're nuts."

We recalled the circumstances of Tommy Cooper's demise in 1984. Midway through his performance in a show televised live before twelve million viewers at Her Majesty's Theatre in London, the red fez-wearing comic genius collapsed from a heart attack and died. The curtains closed awkwardly, and the TV show went to a commercial break. It was bizarre.

Ray enjoyed playing tricks on people. Kathy was a victim of one of his pranks. While she was on holiday in Bali, Ray and two of his mates sneaked into her house and collected all her underwear. When she arrived home, there was a large block of ice waiting for her at her front door. All her undies were inside the block. It took three days for the ice to melt.

Kathy's house party was a lively affair. Everyone gathered in the living room in groups. People chatted aimlessly among themselves. The volume was raised when someone mentioned the front-page report in the *Advertiser*, headlined 'Witnesses heard "I'll stab you".' It gave rise to a prominent member in the community phoning the editor in disgust, saying the report showed "the sensitivity of a wounded buffalo".

Local people in Katherine were uneasy, and curious. They wanted to know all the gory details about the harrowing attack. Did anyone know the alleged killer? Who was the unfortunate victim who got "whacked"? The discussion rambled on with all manner of theory and accusation. No one had answers. And, if they did, they weren't saying.

My effort at pulling a poker face appeared to have saved me. Considering I'd never sat through a poker game in my life, I considered that quite a feat. Then someone spoilt the party for me. He said the article had my byline, so I must have the inside story. No, I protested, smartly. While I reported on the hearing, I knew little about the accused. The argument was cut short, shattered by the unnerving sound of breaking glass. The rumpus allowed me to gingerly dart out of the room unnoticed.

On my way to the toilet, in a darkened hallway, I was lost in thought. A young woman stood against the wall. As she pulled hard on a cigarette, she stumbled slightly. In trying to regain her balance amidst a puff of smoke, she pressed her outstretched hand against my shoulder. It was an act of folly, I assumed, that could befall anyone at a late-night party.

I caught sight of the woman's troubled face, clueless as to who she was. She didn't work at the *Advertiser*, that's for sure. Was she one of Kathy's friends? Or a neighbour, perhaps. On my way back from the bathroom, the woman sat bent over at the foot of the stairs. She turned towards me, and we looked at each other, as strangers do.

She curled her lip, her face showing something beyond disapproval. She moved closer and whispered words in my ear. "Sorry, *what* was that you said?" I asked her gruffly, my heart racing. She stiffened and spoke again, the anger in her voice palpable. She said she was in court for the murder case and had read my report in the newspaper.

It was then that I wished my editor assigned me to cover community events, like celebrations at the School of the Air or the launch of Katherine's local volunteer radio?

She said her sister was the accused's partner. With scowled defiance, she warned me never to walk home late at night. "Girls have balls too you know - they're just higher up," she said, her voice trembling and her breath fuming with alcohol.

She slumped to the ground and began to sob, tears streaming down her face. I showed her the palms of my hands, a gesture intended to signal my desire to avoid a clash - an olive branch. As she fought to get back on her feet, I knew the situation was hopeless; it was time to leave.

From the hallway, I heard howls of laughter coming from the sitting room. I headed for the front door and stepped outside. Walking along the footpath of the unlit road, the screech of an owl rang out. I recall as a boy being told by my father that such a raucous cry after dark was an omen of death, or a future fractured by misfortune.

A nervous chill coursed through my veins. I felt bewitched. If the woman's intention was to scare the bejaysus out of me, she'd made a good fist of it.

When I got home, I went straight to bed. My head lay softly on the pillow, my eyes were closed but I couldn't for the life of me shut out the thoughts from my mind of what had happened earlier.

The next morning over breakfast, I gave Phil a run-down on the night before. He shrugged me off by saying I was blowing everything out of proportion, it was a storm in a teacup. "Well," I replied prickly, "it's a bloody big teacup!"

"Aren't you getting your hair cut today?" he asked. I nodded. "Oh, I'd be worried if I were you," he countered. "What if your new mate works at the salon? Scissors Sister might have a shaky hand!" he said, adding a note of levity, unintentionally but unfortunately. "Always the wise guy!" I shot back, slack jawed.

Phil looked down; his fingers interlaced. He quoted an Al Pacino line from the gangster film *Scarface*: "All I have in this world is my balls and my word – and I don't break them for no one." Balls. Not again! But unlike the tangled threat posed by my testosterone-fuelled assailant the previous night, I trusted it was his way of making light of the darkness.

***

After a year living in the Northern Territory, what I missed most about Ireland - apart from family and friends - was the ocean. Having been fortunate to have grown up beside the sea in Dublin, finding myself plonked in the middle of Australia with only Katherine Gorge as a body of water created a feeling of isolation and claustrophobia. After all, 70 per cent of the planet's surface is covered by ocean. It would have been nice to have seen some of it.

I missed the shoreline; the salty air, sweeping winds and the waves lapping up against the rocks in between tides at the Forty Foot. Oddly enough, I also hankered for a winter swim so bracing that when you submerge into the seven-degree water you get brain freeze. Then, as you resurface, Howth is but a blur above the grand sweep of Dublin Bay.

Katherine Gorge under a clear blue sky in the dry season is spectacularly beautiful, but there were times when I dreamt of being clasped by a winter chill under the umbrella of grey, threatening clouds. How you look at the sea is a distraction for the brain from other more demanding activity. Psychologists call such observation 'soft focus'.

You observe where the tide marks are on the beach, and if the waves are choppy or still. I imagined swimmers pulling their caps down over their plugged ears and immersing themselves in what James Joyce described in *Ulysses* as "the scrotumtightening sea".

The bathers would round the buoys, oblivious to the flight of cormorants close by, ducking and diving for food. In restful moments, when thoughts of the ocean sprung to mind, I consoled myself by whistling a verse of the old English music hall ditty, 'Oh, I Do Like to Be Beside the Seaside'.

The song was written by John H Glover-Kind in 1907, in the days when English people spent their summer holidays in seaside towns like Brighton and Blackpool. The home holidays towered in popularity up until the 1960s when cheap flights were launched, offering packages to 'exotic' Spanish resorts like Magaluf and Benidorm.

Oh! I do like to be beside the seaside!
I do like to be beside the sea!
For the sun's always shining as I make my way
And the brass bands play "Ta-ra-ra-boom-de-ay".
So just let me be beside the seaside!
I'll be beside myself with glee.
And there's lots of girls besides,
I should like to be beside,
beside the seaside, beside the sea!

Chapter 11

Call to Arms

"Getting through life is not a stroll across a field"
– Boris Pasternak

Katherine, March 1989

Situated at the Top End of Australia, Darwin is the State capital closest to Asia and the Pacific Rim. The city is closer to the Indonesian capital of Jakarta than it is to Australia's Federal capital, Canberra. It is about the same flying time from Singapore and Manila as it is from Sydney and Melbourne.

Holidaymakers fly from Darwin to Bali in under three hours. Katherine is about a three-and-half hour drive. To get there, you follow the Stuart Highway, a road which runs south-east for 310 kilometres, passing through the townships of Adelaide River, Burrundie and Pine Creek.

Darwin was named after Charles Darwin in 1839, the British naturalist and geologist who devised the theory of evolution. Perhaps understandably given the restrictions on travel options at the time, he never set foot in the place. Today, Darwin is a shadow of its previous incarnations.

The city and its suburbs were almost entirely rebuilt and reinvented - not once, but four times. What started out as a fledgling settlement was devastated by a cyclone in 1897, a second one in 1937, when it was a colonial capital, followed by a series of Japanese air raids during the Second World War.

In the early hours of Christmas Eve 1974, a small, developing easterly storm looked as though it might pass clear of the Northern Territory. However, the winds turned, and severe tropical Cyclone Tracy headed straight for Darwin.

By 10pm that day, wind gusts got up 217 kilometres per hour (135mph), before instruments failed. The anemometer in Darwin Airport had its needle bent in half by the strength of the gusts. People were getting into party mood for the Christmas celebrations.

Most people did not immediately see it as an emergency, partly because an earlier cyclone safely passed west of the city. News outlets had only skeleton staff on duty over the holiday. The destruction left by Tracy was seismic.

There were 71 people killed, and it caused almost $7 billion in damage in today's money as it levelled about 70 per cent of Darwin's buildings, including 80 per cent of homes. The ruin was etched into the hearts, memories, and blueprint of the city.

Following the bombing of Pearl Harbor by Japanese forces in December 1941, America entered the Second World War. President Franklin D Roosevelt saw Australia as the best place to launch a counter-offensive against the Japanese. General Douglas MacArthur was despatched to Australia, where he was hailed as a hero.

It was the start of a love affair with America and the many wars it would it get dragged into across the world.

American soldiers, known as GIs, showered Australian women with gifts and old-fashioned charm amid cries of "over-paid, over-sexed and over here". Black GIs had to be given special dispensation to enter the country due to Australia's white only policy.

On February 19th, 1942, the Japanese launched a blistering attack on northern Australia. The Bombing of Darwin, also known as the Battle of Darwin, was the biggest single raid ever waged by a foreign power on Australian soil.

The two raids were the first and most destructive air attacks against Australia during the Second World War. They struck just four days after the fall of Singapore, when a combined force surrendered to the Japanese, prompted the biggest concession in the history of the British Empire. The battle-hardened Japanese also bombed Broome and other northern parts of Western Australia.

At the *Katherine Advertiser*, I was given the name of a veteran stationed in Darwin at the time of the Japanese attacks. Roy Waddle was fair dinkum – a true blue Aussie. His father was English, from Hull, and his mother was an Irishwoman who grew up in County Kildare. He told me about that day when 242 Japanese aircraft, in two separate raids, attacked the town centre, several ships moored in the harbour, and local airfields.

The Japanese wanted to stop the Allies from using Darwin as a base for mounting attacks in their bid to seize control of Java in Indonesia and the island of Timor, located about 700 kilometres to the north-west.

"That day, we were like bloody lambs to the slaughter," Roy said with a cool and steady gaze. "When the Japs attacked us, we were caught with our pants down - we weren't prepared." The enemy inflicted heavy losses, at little cost to themselves. The Japanese dropped 683 bombs. Darwin was turned to rubble and dust.

Roy was never the same again either. He was caught up in a bomb blast with shrapnel injuries to his chest and limbs. Shards of metal remained in his left leg. He could hardly stand, never mind walk. He grew ill-tempered and mentally sluggish, a wanderer in a somnambulant world.

In 1951, he moved with his family to Katherine. Roy asked me if I had ever visited Darwin and, if so, what impression did it create. I told him that I'd been there on one occasion for a few days. Despite all the new buildings, I thought the city felt old-worldly.

The abiding memory I had of my time in Darwin was a visit to a crocodile farm and seeing a three-metre albino saltwater croc in an enclosure. An unbelievable-looking creature, it was caught by a fisherman in the nearby Adelaide River.

While tourists are told about the city's balmy weather and outdoor life, I was unnerved by how many poisonous snakes were at home there. Down by the waterfront, from October to May, there are signs warning people not to swim in the sea due to the threat posed by crocodiles, sharks, box jellyfish and the extremely venomous blue-ringed octopus.

Arachnophobes beware! The Territory is spared clusters of the highly poisonous funnel-web spider found on the east coast, but they have the redback which lurks in dry, dark spaces and whose bite can cause nausea or headache. Antivenom normally quells the effects. Most of the other spiders found in the Top End are harmless.

Somewhere between 250 and 300 people were killed and another 400 wounded in the two Japanese raids on Darwin. Most of the dead were soldiers. Nine ships in the harbour and two anchored in the waters outside it were sunk. Another twenty-five vessels were damaged.

The local airfield came under fire too, with thirty planes destroyed, along with a host of civil facilities in the city centre. More than half of Darwin's population left just before or immediately after the Japanese attacks, never to return.

What occurred in the Top End during the Second World War had links to the Royal Australian Air Force (RAAF) base, situated 15 kilometres south-east of Katherine. The base was first built as Carson's Airfield by the US Army 43rd Engineer General Service Regiment in 1942, to provide a facility for heavy bombers striking Japanese targets in Papua New Guinea and the Dutch East Indies.

However, as the tide turned during the Second World War, there was no need for aircraft to use the base. After the war ended in 1946, the airfield was renamed Tindal, in honour of wing commander Archibald 'Archie' Tindal, the first RAAF member killed in action on the Australian mainland during the war.

Archie Tindal died while manning a machine gun against Japanese soldiers bombing Darwin in February 1942. He was buried at the Adelaide River war cemetery.

Australians are no strangers to fighting other nations' wars, and seeing their soldiers return home in body bags. It created a miasma of despair and outrage among many Aussies, as they believed that the contribution their soldiers made to the war effort was less valued than other Allied forces.

In 1915, in the First World War, around 16,000 soldiers from Australia and New Zealand, known as Anzacs, landed on the beaches at Gallipoli, in what is now Turkey. It was the 'diggers' first experience of combat. On the first day, 2,000 of them were killed or wounded. When the battle finally ended, as many as 11,000 soldiers are said to have lost their lives, an exercise which some observers compared to "shooting fish in a barrel".

The worst year for Anzacs engaged on the Western Front was 1917. An unprecedented scale of death and destruction resulted in 76,000 Australian casualties, which included the four-month long Battle of Passchendaele.

Enlistments began to flag. The British wanted 5,500 Australian soldiers a month to sign up. The Federal government in Canberra tried to introduce mandatory enlistment but the proposal was voted down. Munition factories and comfort parcels for soldiers provided jobs for Australian women for the first time.

Call to Arms

When the war finally ended in 1918, Australia had paid a high price, with 60,000 of their soldiers dead and 150,000 wounded or taken prisoner from the almost 417,000 men enlisted.

The 65 per cent mortality rate was the highest of any Allied nation in the war. The Aboriginal soldiers who fought for their country were denied the war pensions that were given to white Australians.

An excerpt from 'Waltzing Matilda'...

Well, I remember that terrible day
When our blood stained the sand and the water
And how in that hell that they called Suvla Bay
We were butchered like lambs at the slaughter.

Johnny Turk he was ready
Oh he primed himself well.
He rained us with bullets,
And he showered us with shells.

And in five minutes flat,
We were all blown to hell
Nearly blew us back home to Australia.

Around one million Australian soldiers fought in the Second World War. Of them, 27,000 were killed in action, and almost the same number wounded. Of the 22,000 wounded, one in three died or were captured by the Japanese and held as prisoners of war. About 17,000 Australian soldiers fought in Korea between 1950 and 1953, with casualties numbering 339 dead and 1,200 wounded.

Australia was one of only five nations that sent combat troops to help America try to defeat North Vietnamese forces and the southern-based Viet Cong insurgency. US president Lyndon Johnson wanted to form an international alliance, but America's traditional allies - Britain, France, and Canada - refused to get involved and instead called for peace talks.

From 1962, 60,000 Australian soldiers, including ground troops and air and navy personnel, served in Vietnam. As many as 523 combatants died and 2,400 were wounded. A total of 58,200 American soldiers died. As many as two million Vietnamese civilians on both sides were killed. An estimated 1.1 million North Vietnamese and Viet Cong soldiers perished, and 250,000 South Vietnamese combatants lost their lives.

The Anzacs' special operators had a reputation of bravery and reputation. By 1969, the number of anti-war protests had spiralled, as more Australians came to believe the war could not be won.

Many of those who signed up to fight in Vietnam felt they were looked down upon by their fellow compatriots. On their return home, soldiers were spat at in public, having served in what some believed to be not "a proper war".

Half a century on from Australia's final role in the war in 1973, the Returned & Services League of Australia (RSL) charity made a formal apology about the way its soldiers were treated. The RSL, which provides support for veterans who served in the Australian Defence Force (ADF), accepted they had made grave errors. Medals for gallantry were awarded posthumously.

In 1963, following a review, it was decided to upgrade the Tindal airfield as Australia's defences in the north of the country needed strengthening. The airfield was close enough to RAAF Base Darwin to afford mutual protection, but far enough from the coast to be defensible and avoid the effects of tropical cyclones. Katherine was also outside the projected fall-out zone should Darwin be targeted by a nuclear weapon, and the area boasted adequate water supply and transport links.

In 1984, the Australian government moved the RAAF's fleet of fighter aircraft in the Northern Territory from Darwin to Tindal. Four years later, the base was made fully operational and became Australia's first manned RAAF base to be rolled out since the Second World War. Labor prime minister Bob Hawke and defence minister Kim Beazley performed the honours in March 1989.

****

In 1999, the RAAF base at Tindal near Katherine supported the intervention during the East Timorese struggle for independence with Australian F-111s and Skyhawks armed and on standby to attack Indonesian forces and command systems. The base also helped with exercises during the invasion of Iraq in 2003.

In more recent years, the US has committed funds for a further upgrade, with an expanded apron allowing space for six B-52 bombers with nuclear capabilities. The move provoked controversy in Australia amid worries of heightening tension with China.

The RAAF responded to public unease by claiming that American bombers have been stationed in Australia since the 1980s and took part in training exercises since 2005. Tindal is the permanent home of a F-35A stealth fighter squadron. The cost of modernising the military and civil aviation base is expected to be around $100 million when it's completed in 2026.

Australia has signed an agreement with the US and the UK to create a new fleet of nuclear-powered submarines, aimed at countering China's influence in the Indo-Pacific region. The deal proved highly divisive as France expected to be awarded the contract.

Under the Aukus pact, Australia will get its first nuclear-powered subs - at least three - from the US. The allies will also work to create a new fleet using cutting-edge tech, including UK-made Rolls-Royce reactors. Beijing condemned the naval deal, with its foreign ministry accusing the three nations of "walking further and further down the path of error and danger".

China's UN mission accused the Western allies of setting back nuclear non-proliferation efforts. But US president Joe Biden said the deal was aimed at bolstering peace in the region and stressed the submarines would be "nuclear-powered, not nuclear-armed".

From 2027, the US and UK will also base a small number of nuclear submarines in Perth before Canberra will buy three US-model Virginia-class submarines in the early 2030s - with options to purchase two more.

After that, the plan is to design and build an entirely new nuclear-powered submarine for the UK and Australian forces - a model that is being called SSN-Aukus. The attack craft will be built in the UK and Australia to a British design, using technology from all three countries.

Australia plans to start manufacturing its own missiles by 2026. The *Sydney Morning Herald* reported that the plan will allow the country to supply guided weapons to the US and other nations. The move was driven by Russia's invasion of Ukraine in early 2022, which highlighted a troubling lack of ammunition stocks among Nato members.

Chapter 12

Football Crazy

"The more difficult the victory, the greater the happiness in winning" – Edson Arantes do Nascimento, aka Pelé

Fremantle, May 1989

At the end of April 1989, I decided it was time to leave the Northern Territory and return to Western Australia. After applying for several jobs, I was fortunate to secure an editorial position with a publisher in Perth. The company, Associated Media, produced a stable of periodicals in the fields of tourism and horticulture. The flagship title was called *All About Town*, a 'priceless' glossy fortnightly specialising in the hospitality industry.

Mostly, I'd travel from Freo to the office in Subiaco by train. Occasionally, I'd cycle the 20 kilometres there, lured by the breathtaking views of the Swan River. My helmet was fitted with cable ties to deter swooping magpies during the nesting season. The black and white stealth bombers attack cyclists out of fear they might pose a threat to their chicks.

My boss, Ron Spencer, had an encyclopaedic knowledge of fine cuisine, and he was generous with it. He was razor-sharp and loved a good yarn. He knew all the best places to dine in Western Australia, and well beyond. His contact list across restaurants, hotels, and food and wine producers was extraordinary. He spoke at length about classic and New World wines.

Over a bottle of sparking shiraz from the Barossa Valley, Ron told me about how wines were getting stronger. As the world climates warm up, grapes were ripening with higher sugar levels. Fermented sugar is what creates the alcohol. As the planet keeps warming up, the potency of wines will increase. A limit will be reached as yeast only ferments up to about 16 per cent alcohol by volume (ABV).

It was while we were having lunch in Perth's Hyatt Hotel that I overheard two English tourists in conversation. They were talking football, and how they planned to stay up late into the night to watch a "big match" on TV in the hotel. It was so fortuitous, a 'heads up' on a Friday afternoon as I learnt that 'my team' Arsenal were about to play in a game to decide who wins the English league title.

It was May 26th, 1989, about four years before the world wide web came into general use. It meant staying up until 3am to watch 22 men kicking around a bladder in a bag for 90 or so minutes on a damp Friday night in Liverpool. But this was no ordinary football match. It was an end of season contest to decide the winner of the 1988/'89 Barclays League Championship.

Reigning champions Liverpool were hosting Arsenal, "my heroes", at Anfield. Leading the league by three points, the home side were on the brink of achieving the double, having won the FA Cup by defeating Merseyside rivals Everton 3-2 at Wembley six days earlier. To be crowned double winners, the Reds must draw, win, or lose the match by just one goal.

Arsenal, on the other hand, had dropped vital points in recent games against Derby County and Wimbledon. The Gunners had to win at Anfield by at least two clear goals. The teams were level on points and goal difference, but Arsenal would edge it if they won two-nil as they had scored more goals during the season than the Scousers.

The clash was delicately poised. A standalone game, a cup final in all but name. Home alone in Fremantle and perched on the edge of the couch, I switched on the television and watched nervously as Liverpool players reverentially touched the 'This is Anfield' sign and ran out on to the pitch.

The atmosphere was electric.

The stadium was heaving.

I felt a shiver of goosebumps on my neck as the Liverpool anthem, 'You'll Never Walk Alone', rang out from The Kop. A sea of red scarves and flags swayed in slow motion. The punters gave Arsenal little chance of victory. Miracles don't happen, I thought to myself, or do they?

The sports pages in the *Daily Mirror* that day led with the headline 'You Haven't Got a Prayer, Arsenal'. The team's manager George Graham compared the challenge facing his team at Anfield that night to "climbing a mountain". Renowned for his insistence on a defiant back line, he saw the Liverpool threat coming from out wide. The wings and prayers are what Arsenal needed.

As the team sheets showed up on the screen, the voice of ITV commentator Brian Moore announced the news that Arsenal would play a 5-4-1 formation, with Lee Dixon and Nigel Winterburn as full-backs, captain Tony Adams and Steve Bould (wearing number ten) as centre backs, and David O'Leary as sweeper.

In the run-up to kick-off, every player on the Arsenal team presented bouquets of flowers to home supporters in memory of the 97 Liverpool fans who lost their lives at the Hillsborough stadium in Sheffield five weeks before. Liverpool manager Kenny Dalglish and several of his players expressed their appreciation at the gesture.

Following a short delay due to traffic congestion in the city, the match started at 8.05pm local time. In the first half, Arsenal appeared cautious. At the interval, it was still scoreless. As the second half got underway, Liverpool seemed quietly confident about holding on.

With 52 minutes on the clock, Arsenal were awarded a free kick wide on the right. Kevin Richardson crossed the ball high into the box. Alan Smith was there to meet it and head past Liverpool goalkeeper Bruce Grobbelaar.

Liverpool players appealed to the referee. Offside, they shouted. Others claimed that the ball went in without Smith getting the required touch. Or that there was a push by David O'Leary. Straws and grasping came to mind. The referee waved away the protests. He pointed to the half-way line. One-nil to the Arsenal.

The game went on, with the Gunners battling away but still needing a second goal without reply to win the game – and, crucially, secure the league title. As the stalemate intensified, the tempo flagged further. The quicks on my fingernails came under growing pressure. I had to contain myself from firing something, anything at all, at the TV.

With normal time almost up, Liverpool midfielder Steve McMahon raised one finger to signal to his teammates they only needed to hang on for a minute. Liverpool went on the attack down the left-hand side, as John Barnes's run was intercepted. Arsenal 'keeper David Lukic threw the ball out to Lee Dixon on the right, and play moved into the Liverpool half.

Alan Smith flicked the ball on as Mickey Thomas charged through the centre of midfield. It looked as though Ray Houghton might get a tackle in or bring Thomas down in the box. He did neither. Thomas got a shot off and it ended up in the back of the Liverpool net. Arsenal had scored again. It was unreal!

They had climbed the mountain, scaled new heights, and the summit flag was within sight.

As the ref blew the final whistle, Arsenal's fans, known as Gooners, looked towards the heavens, their prayers answered. The players on both teams were stunned. On the sideline, Arsenal's Niall Quinn jumped up and down and hugged everyone he could grab. "Boring, boring Arsenal" had done it. Not one-nil; but two-nil, as required.

Former American football quarterback Joe Namath once said: "When you win, nothing hurts." He wasn't wrong. Not so for the vanquished. David O'Leary went to comfort Liverpool striker John Aldridge as he sat hunched on the pitch. The two players were Republic of Ireland teammates and friends. Aldridge was crestfallen. The shock of losing a hugely important match in such circumstances was too much, too soon.

The Arsenal players applauded and waved to their fans, some of whom shed tears of joy.

A jubilant Tony Adams lifted the trophy, before escorting his teammates to the dressing room to get the champagne celebrations flowing. When the Gunners won the double in 1971, George Graham was an Arsenal player. Now, he was 'the gaffer' - the boss.

Lee Dixon later said in an interview that Graham instilled "an inner belief" in the players that they could defy the odds and win at Anfield. Winning goal scorer Mickey Thomas described the victory as "an out-of-body experience".

In Australia, Channel Seven News later showed jubilant Arsenal fans streaming into Highbury Stadium from seven in the morning. The ground was full to overflowing with more than 38,000 Gooners. A quarter of a million well-wishers lined the streets of North London as the Arsenal team paraded the trophy from an open top bus.

A civic reception was held at Islington Town Hall. David O'Leary had to miss out on the post-match celebrations. He was on a plane to Dublin, where he would join up with the rest of Jack Charlton's Republic of Ireland squad.

At six o'clock on that Saturday morning I felt exceptional, yet lonely. On top of the world, but embedded in Western Australia, almost 15,000 kilometres from home. Arsenal were league champions, a feat achieved in the most incredible way, and all I wanted to do was celebrate wildly. To share the elation with others. In my dreams.

Rather than retire to bed, I watched TV and prepared breakfast. That morning it finally dawned on me how none of the TV stations in Australia could come next or near the BBC in terms of quality programming. Along with the best shows RTÉ offered, Irish viewers didn't realise how lucky they were compared to TV audiences elsewhere in the world.

In the days ahead, no one I met in Perth had a notion of what Arsenal had achieved. Why would they? In 1992, *Fever Pitch*, Nick Hornby's page-turning autobiography on the ecstasy (infrequent) and heartache (frequent) of being a Gooner, made amends. It told the story of the title decider with aplomb. More than a million copies were sold in the UK.

A mountain of books.

Chapter 13

Titan of Wit

"Words are to be spent. They are the currency of the mind"
– Saul Bellow

Perth, May 1989

They say you should never meet your heroes; it only ends in disappointment. However, I couldn't resist the opportunity of a once-in-a lifetime, face-to-face chat with the TV host who slagged his guests with the passion of an evangelist - but never mocked. A writer magisterial for his erudition. I had an interview lined up with Clive James, a man who could make cobwebs with words.

The interview was in Burswood Island, a sprawling hotel resort three kilometres outside Perth's general business district. Lying on the banks of the Swan River, Burswood comprised a casino, convention centre with meeting rooms, a theatre and two ballrooms along with 32 restaurants and bars, a nightclub, and several upmarket hotels.

The brainchild of local businessman Dallas Dempster and Malaysian casino operator Genting Berhad, the resort became the largest gambling den in Australia and the third biggest in the world – no mean feat for a site that started out as a rubbish tip and cement works. Burswood was expected to open in time for the America's Cup in Fremantle in 1987. Due to unforeseen delays, the launch was held over until early the following year.

In more recent years, the casino was embroiled in a series of controversies, including allegations of money laundering and the flouting of Covid-19 lockdown rules. Concerns about problem gambling were heightened after financial reports were published showing $306 million was gambled in a year on the casino's 2,500 gaming machines.

In March 2022, Crown Resorts escaped having its casino licence cancelled. The Perth Casino Royal Commission gave it two years to get its house in order under the supervision of an independent monitor.

The general manager set aside a guest room near the hotel's conference centre for our interview. I arrived about ten minutes early, an opportunity to check my notes. James walked through the door right on time. I had butterflies in my stomach, but my interviewee's open-hearted smile and outgoing demeanour vanquished my nerves.

I introduced myself. James immediately began by recalling his visits to Ireland. He talked about the time he was a guest of Gay Byrne on the *Late Late Show*. He riffed on about how intrigued he was by Irish people's creative use of the English language. "I just love your guys' lingo," he said in his signature Aussie drawl.

"You say things like 'eejit'... 'you're a terrible eejit'." I assured him that while the word was a derivative of idiot, it also served as a term of endearment, in the same way as a bloke in Australia might call someone 'a bastard' – it depends on the context. He recalled Flann O'Brien's *At Swim-Two-Birds* and laughing aloud when the word 'banjaxed' jumped off the page at him.

As for "you're grand", if he heard it once, he heard it a thousand times. He was baffled by "sure, you won't know yourself". He was fascinated by how Irish people could start a sentence with "Come here..." followed by "now, wait 'til I tell you..." In a café in Galway, he overheard a woman chatting to a friend and starting every sentence with "shurelookit".

He recounted a visit he made to Cork and how local people there loved saying "ye". One evening, he was having a drink in Costigan's pub on Washington Street, and he got chatting to a local man at the bar. "Would I be right in thinking you're not from this neck of the woods?" the Corkonian asked. Before James could reply, the man added: "See that langer over there. That's Miah. It's not a chip he has on his shoulder, it's a frying pan!"

Irish signposts aroused his curiosity. Placenames like Swanlinbar in Cavan and Nobber in County Meath. And Cork's Ballydehob, where he enjoyed a music session in Rosie's Bar. One day, he was 'taken' to Hospital in County Limerick and drove past Bastardstown in County Wexford. He learned that Muckanaghederdauhaulia, near Galway, was Ireland's longest one-word placename. It roughly translates from Irish as "a pig marsh between two seas".

"In Australia," James said, "we've a heap of weird placenames. In Sydney, there's Barangaroo. Up the way is Wagga Wagga." I mentioned to him that while living in the Northern Territory, I came across a small town near Darwin popular with tourists which was immortalised in bush ballads by Slim Dusty and Ted Egan. The place is known as Humpty Doo. "That's a keeper!" he said with a guffaw.

His favourite TV personality was Dave Allen, the Irishman whose real name was David Tynan O'Mahony. Humour and acting the clown was in his genes. I shared a few yarns with him about Allen's father, which might have helped explain why his son ended up a comedian. Gerard Tynan O'Mahony, a Limerickman, was general manager at *The Irish Times* in the late 1940s. He was an eccentric.

One night, he returned to work at the newspaper office having over-imbibed in a nearby bar. He was spotted by a colleague down on all fours sipping milk from a saucer left out for the works cat. His caper earned him the nickname 'Pussy' O'Mahony.

There was the night when he took a short cut to his home in south Dublin. Along the way, he fell into a freshly dug grave, but because of his wooden leg he couldn't climb out. A second person joined him in the hole. O'Mahony roared in the darkness: "You'll never get out of here!". The man jumped out of the hole and scarpered. On another occasion, he went to a fancy-dress ball disguised as a toffee apple.

James first moved to London in 1962 from the Sydney suburb of Kogarah. He was joined in England by a handful of his compatriots, including writer and feminist Germaine Greer, and art critic and TV producer Robert Hughes. Melbourne-born comedian Barry Humphries was also among the Aussie clan that moved to England. His alter egos included the drunk diplomat Sir Les Paterson and - more famously - Dame Edna Everage, whose trademark greeting was "Hello possums!"

Humphries described the Edna shows as "a monologue interrupted by strangers" and 'herself' as blessed with a knack to laugh at the misfortune of others. In stark contrast with James, the drag star's TV performance relied on a preference to warmly skewer celebrities and audience members alike.

James graduated in English and psychology from the University of Sydney. He attended Pembroke College Cambridge where he read English literature. In 1968, he appeared on *University Challenge*. His contemporaries at the university included Germaine Greer, historian Simon Schama and Monty Python's Eric Idle.

Another famous Australian who emigrated to England a decade before was Rolf Harris. A native of Perth, 'the boy from Balga' arrived in London in 1952 at the age of 22. He attended art school and went on to become a TV star.

His talents ranged from singing ('Tie Me Kangaroo Down, Sport' and 'Two Little Boys'), musician (didgeridoo) and art (fun art and a portrait of Queen Elizabeth). By accident, he invented a musical instrument called the wobble board. However, Harris himself later suffered a major wobble in his life – which was not invented and was no accident.

In 2013, he was arrested as part of Operation Yewtree, the police investigation launched following the Jimmy Savile sex abuse scandal. A year later, he was found guilty of twelve counts of indecent assault on girls aged between 14 and 16. He was sentenced to five years and nine months in prison. Released on licence in 2017, he died at his home in May 2023, aged 93. News of his death was delayed for two weeks to allow him "a dignified funeral".

James told me that the Australian he admired most was Carmen Callil. She shook up the stuffy world of British media by launching the feminist publishing house Virago Press in 1973 and opened doors for a long line of gifted writers, including Irish scribes Mary Lavin, Maura Laverty and Kate O'Brien and Molly Keane. She and novelist Polly Devlin were trusted friends for half a century.

Callil's forbears had emigrated to Australia from Ireland and Lebanon and settled in Melbourne. Despite her reputation of being caustic, argumentative and needy, James regarded her as formidable, fearless, and unflinchingly loyal. He saw her as someone who was fixed on leaving her mark on the literary world and to live her life the way she wanted by coming out of the shadows.

In 1985, Callil helped launch the Groucho Club, the louche private members' club for arts and media publishers in London's Soho district. She went on to write two highly-acclaimed moral books – *Bad Faith* and *Oh Happy Day*. She was made a dame, got awarded the coveted Benson Medal from the Royal Society of Literature, sat on the board of Channel 4, and served on the Booker Prize committee.

James said he enjoyed going to dinner parties hosted by writer Gita Mehta. As an author, Mehta presented a nuanced portrait of her native India – even though she had no intention of being a writer. One evening, a guest grabbed her sari, pulled her into his group and said she was the girl who was going to explain to them what karma was all about.

The invited guest was Marc Jaffe, editorial director at Random Penguin's Bantam Books. He was responsible for commissioning one of the most famous books of the 1980s. Mehta's *Karma Cola – Marketing the Mystic East*, which was published by Simon & Schuster in 1979, was a collection of anecdotes about the Western travellers she met in India. The book took a sceptical but amusing line on India's flourishing guru industry and the hippies who flocked there for their fix of spiritual opium. Mehta wrote: "Everyone suspected that whatever America wanted, America got. Why not Nirvana?"

James earned global recognition as a TV host, raconteur, newspaper columnist and writer of books. However, some people may have been less aware that he was also a lover of poetry, not least WB Yeats, Robert Frost and Philip Larkin. His collection of verses was published under the title *Poetry Notebook*.

He was a member of Mensa and a polymath, but he seemed decidedly unsettled when I mentioned it. He taught himself French by reading Marcel Proust novels with a dictionary, joking that he may have forgotten to say it took him fifteen years. He was chuffed that he could converse in Russian, Japanese, German and Italian.

James spoke about being a fan of Dorothy Parker. When the American poet and wit was told the 1920s US president Calvin Coolidge had just died, she famously remarked: "How can they tell?" Ironically, for someone who wrote voluminously, his favourite Parker line was: "I hate writing, I love having written". Yet, he wasn't blinded by his admiration for her.

Being an admirer of smart women like Jackie Kennedy-Onassis and Diane Keaton, he saw no basis for her rhyming line: "Men seldom make passes at girls who wear glasses."

When pressed to name which of his books he enjoyed writing the most, he singled out *From the Land of Shadows*, his 1982 collection of literary-critical essays brim full of wit. In the book's introduction, he noted: "Literature says most things itself, when it is allowed to."

Clive wasn't his real name. When he was born, his mother called him Vivian after an Australian Davis Cup tennis player from 1938. He believed that the name Vivian, no matter how it was spelt or even when it was shortened to Viv, would forever be synonymous with Vivien Leigh, the actress who starred opposite Clark Gable in *Gone with the Wind*. He changed his name to Clive, after Tyrone Power's character in the 1942 film, *This Above All*.

As he wrote in *Unreliable Memoirs* (1979), the name chosen for him by his parents could have been considerably worse. What if he ended up like the Australian boy whose father, a soldier, named him after the campaigns he fought in the Egyptian desert? The lad went by the name of William Bardia Escarpment Qattara Depression Mersa Matruh El Alamein Benghazi Tripoli Harris.

James's father died when he was six years old, and his mother never got over the loss. "I am trying to lead the life they might have had," he said about his parents in an interview several years later. "It's a chance to pay them back for my life. I don't like luck; I've had a lot of it."

He thrived on presenting travel postcards from the world's major cities. In 1988, the BBC offered him the chance to present the seven-part travel series, *Around the World in Eighty Days*, a re-enactment of the Jules Vernes picaresque novel of the same name. However, it would have meant him crossing the globe without flying, so he declined the invite; Michael Palin got the gig and followed in the footsteps of Phileas Fogg.

James enjoyed poking fun at *Endurance*, the sadistic Japanese TV game show that ran long before reality TV assaulted the airwaves. Contestants were buried up to their neck, bitten by ants and licked by lizards. As he noted in the introduction to his book, *Glued to the Box,* a collection of TV reviews he wrote for the *Observer*: "Anyone afraid of what he thinks television does to the world is probably just afraid of the world."

He was a big fan of motor racing. He counted Formula 1 supremo Bernie Ecclestone among his closest friends. He presented a host and videos and season review shows.

Of all the cities in the world, Paris was the one he held dearest. He was enchanted by its elan and the grandeur of the city's Haussmann-style architecture. His favourite café was on the other side of the Rue de l'Université from the boutique hotel where he always stayed.

He'd sit there for hours, reading his way through a pile of novels he had just bought from the green book boxes dotted along the Seine. He made notes and occasionally might start writing a new book. "That's my Paris," he said, "and it's every writer's Paris who has been there. I can remember everything, except the name of the café."

James was married to Australian author Prue Shaw. The relationship was overshadowed by infidelity, and they got divorced in 2012, but they remained friends. He endured a long and exhausting battle with leukaemia and developed kidney failure and a serious lung condition.

He died peacefully at his home in Cambridge in November 2019, aged 80. He had asked that at the end of his funeral service they play the Eric Carmen song 'All By Myself'. Despite valiant efforts, I was unable to determine if his request was granted.

The interview with Clive James was published in the *All About Town* newspaper. Right beside the article, an ad appeared inviting readers to enter a competition for cinema tickets to an advanced screening of Jim Sheridan's *My Left Foot*. Based on Irish writer Christy Brown's autobiography, the film went on to win Daniel Day-Lewis the first of his record three best actor Academy Awards. Brenda Fricker became Ireland's first Oscar winner, taking home the best supporting actress statuette for her role as Brown's mother.

The preview, organised with the film's distributors, attracted a full house in a city centre cinema. Before the feature started, I took to the stage and explained to the audience some of the background to the film which was told from the perspective of the acclaimed writer and artist born with cerebral palsy into a working-class Dublin family. His left foot was the only part of his body he could control.

Day-Lewis was the archetypal method actor. He demanded that everyone on set address him as 'Christy'. He ignored anyone who called him 'Daniel'. Such was his physical dedication to the role; he learned to type and paint with his feet just like his character and demanded to be pushed around in a wheelchair.

His refusal to leave his wheelchair meant that the film's production assistants had to lift the actor over all the studio equipment to get him ready for the next scene. Day-Lewis took his obsession a step further during lunch breaks. Set assistants were obliged to spoon-feed him in the same way as Christy's mother did.

As the film's final credits rolled, a spontaneous round of applause rang out in the cinema. It was particularly gratifying to be Irish that night.

When I arrived home in Fremantle later that night, I turned on the TV for the Channel Nine news. I watched with interest as a report from China showed scenes in Beijing's Tiananmen Square where student protestors had gathered for a major sit-in. They had hopes of negotiating with the government in a bid to achieve political reform.

While major demonstrations of civil resistance often spark scenes of violence and chaos in China, there appeared to be a calmness about the students' revolt that was reminiscent of Mahatma Gandhi's peaceful uprisings against British colonial rule in India and his famous 240-mile protest march against salt taxes back in 1930.

By the end of May, one million people had amassed in dissent in Tiananmen Square. As the police and military presence around them intensified, some activists feared the army was getting ready to move in to vacate the square and were prepared to adopt ruthless tactics to bring the protest to an end.

In the early hours of June 4th, troops marched in, opening fire on the students. Tanks flattened tents with sleeping protestors inside and blocked exit routes. Soldiers arrested anyone who tried to flee. Officials claimed 200 protestors were killed that day; student leaders estimated the figure at up to 2,000.

On the following day, a photo of an unidentified man standing alone in the square in front of a row of tanks proved to be one of the most iconic images of the last century. He became known simply as Tank Man. The photo almost never happened.

Associated Press photographer Jeff Widener had flu and was concussed from a blow to the head he incurred the night before. One of his cameras was destroyed. He then ran out of film. He just about managed to get a roll from an American exchange student from whose hotel balcony he took the immortal photos.

Chapter 14

Mercurial Artist

"All the variety, all the charm, all the beauty is made up of light and shadow" - Leo Tolstoy

Perth, July 1989

Pantjiti Mary McLean was said to have been born sometime between 1928 and 1930. Like many Aboriginals at the time, Mary was unsure about her exact birthdate. She knew for definite the place she was born, in the desert south of Ayers Rock. In 1993, Ayers Rock was officially renamed Uluru. The word 'Uluru' is a proper noun from the Pitjantjatjara language and doesn't have an English translation.

A Ngaatjatjarra woman, Mary had little or no contact with 'whitefella' settlement growing up. Her ancestral home was Kaltukatjara, 670 kilometres south-west of Alice Springs, on the Western Australia-Northern Territory border. It also went by the settler's name of Docker River, thanks to an expedition undertaken by Ernest Giles in 1872.

Due to a prolonged drought in the late 1940s and early 1950s, Mary, along with her husband, her son, and many others of her people, were ordered to walk several hundred kilometres from the Western Desert, via the Warburton Ranges, and on to the settlement of Cosmo Newbury in the Eastern Goldfields. From here, they made their way to Laverton, a town in the Goldfields-Esperance region of north WA, which, in 1898, the settlers named British Flag.

By the early 1940s, Government policy dictated that any local Aboriginal children were to be raised and schooled by Evangelical missionaries at the Mount Margaret Mission, located 230 kilometres north-east of the famous gold mining town of Kalgoorlie. The mission was started in 1921 by Rodolphe Samuel Schenk with support from the Australian Aborigines Mission.

Initially rolled out as a refuge for the people of the surrounding area, by the end of the decade Schenk's ethos had diversified with the creation of a school, dormitories and arts and crafts in keeping with his own brand of religion, education, and enterprise. People were soon drawn to the mission from as far east as the Aboriginal community of Warburton, just south of the Gibson Desert - and to the north from the small town of Wiluna, located in the mid-west region on the edge of the Western Desert.

For over half a century, countless families would 'sit down' at the mission, some for a short time, building huts and fences, shepherding goats, and shearing sheep, while others stayed on more permanently - like Mary's family. However, Schenk's policy of paying low wages annoyed local pastoralists as the custom of raising goats relied on help from Aboriginals, many of whom favoured the traditional nomadic lifestyle.

The pastoralists tried to sabotage the mission and have it relocated in the desert. Schenk clashed with Aboriginal elders who accused him of failing to appreciate their traditions. He also had run-ins with political and academic influencers on the contentious issue of how to assimilate Aboriginal people and culture into white society.

For many years, discrimination was tolerated with the widespread use of racist slurs like 'blackfellas', 'abos' and 'darkies', and the perpetrators washed in this shame for decades.

Many youngsters were forcibly removed from their families and sent to the mission in line with Federal government policy, while others were placed there by parents, not always aware of the repercussions. In some instances, entire families were admitted. From an historical perspective, it is generally acknowledged that Mount Margaret was more caring and progressive than other missions in Australia.

The forced migration of Aboriginals to missions first began back in 1901 when Australia became a federal nation within the British Commonwealth. Aboriginals were denied citizenship in their own country and were subjected to human rights abuses.

Almost the entire Aboriginal population of Victoria were relocated to missions where the men were trained as station hands. It was the start of the scandal of what became known as the 'Stolen Generations'.

Mary McLean's son was taken into Mount Margaret. Parents there were directed to find work on the district sheep stations. However, instead of doing the domestic duties most women undertook at the time, Mary chose to work outdoors with the men in the mission. She became an able horse rider and musterer. After several years, she quit station life and worked in the sandalwood camps in Kalgoorlie, up until the time she retired.

Mary then embraced Aboriginal art. Her start in painting was born at a street art project in 1992 run by fibre artist and sculptor Nalda Searles for people from Ninga Mia and other fringe camp communities at Kalgoorlie. Searles' exhibition, 'Drifting in My Own Land', famously toured 18 venues across Australia from 2009 to 2013. The aim of the project was for Aboriginal people of all ages to express themselves through art as a strengthening of cultural values.

Her paintings and prints are everyday narratives evoking the life of her early childhood with energy and abundance: men hunting, women and kids collecting bush tucker or running free, and everyday family life around the camp. She worked in acrylics and watercolours.

The secular and the sacred are enmeshed in her images. The affirmation of life in her work, along with her own, inimitable style, guaranteed her a strong buying public. In 2001, Perth's Curtin University awarded Mary an honorary doctorate for her contribution to the art world and Australia's broader community.

From the time I first saw her paintings, Mary's life and work intrigued me and left a lasting imprint. Eight years later, while on a return visit to WA, I popped into the Desert Design shop on High Street in Fremantle, later renamed the Japingka Gallery. While browsing through the store, I happened upon a painting that stood out from the other exhibits.

The story behind Mary's 'Dogs Fighting Over a Bone' painting is of two men out hunting for kangaroo. Once the roo had been eaten by the men, the camp dogs were thrown the scraps. Two dogs fought over a bone near a waterhole frequented by white cockatoos.

There's an artistry to things that are done well.

Art can give insights into other faiths and cultures. Mary's phantasmagorical images burst with exuberance. Someone once remarked that "one can sense her brush still dancing around the edges". It bears the sacred colours given to Aboriginals during the Dreamtime - black, red, yellow, and white.

Black represents the earth, marking the campfires of the Dreamtime ancestors. Red represents fire, energy, and blood, known as 'djang', a power found in places Aboriginals consider sacred. Yellow is the life-giving sun most often associated with women's ceremonies. White symbolises the sky and stars, filled with the ancestors who returned to the sky after creating the earth.

For many Aboriginals, traditional ochre colours have a spiritual meaning and application. Many ochre deposits are associated with totemic beings. For example, many red ochre sites symbolise the blood of the totemic kangaroo or emu. The pure white clay in western Arnhem Land is said to be the faeces of the great Ngalyod serpent.

When Mungo Man was discovered in south-western New South Wales in 1974, he was found lying on his back with a covering of red ochre. The ochre, which dated back over 40,000 years, was not found in that locality.

Each ochre colour is associated with quite specific meaning and use. Red ochre is often used where conflict prevails, as well as celebration and ceremony. Black pigment is usually derived from coal.

1992 was the year that Mary's artistic talent came to the fore. McLean was soon represented in many high-profile public and private collections in Australia. She won the 1995 Telstra National Aboriginal Art Award and was the commissioned artist for the 1996 Festival of Perth. Her work has been exhibited internationally, including in a retrospective at Australia House in London in 1995.

Perhaps one day, someone will have the foresight to erect a statue in Mary McLean's honour.

Chapter 15

"Man, Overboard Portside!"

Fremantle, November 1989

"The wonder is always new that any sane man can be a sailor" – Ralph Waldo Emerson

1969 was an historic year in sailing. It was the year that British merchant marine officer Robin Knox-Johnston made history by becoming the first man to complete a non-stop, single-handed circumnavigation of the world by winning the *Sunday Times* Golden Globe Race. His achievement planted an idea in the minds of two men which changed the face of offshore racing.

Race promoter Guy Pearce and Anthony Churchill, an ocean sailor and publisher of the *Yachting and Boating Weekly* magazine, were impressed by Knox-Johnson's feat. It convinced them that a crewed race following the old square rigger routes around the world had promise. They believed that the body logistically most qualified to run the race was the Royal Naval Sailing Association (RNSA).

In 1971, retired British Navy officer Admiral Otto Steiner, acting for the RNSA, met with Colonel Bill Whitbread of the brewing family over a beer in a smoke-filled bar in Portsmouth, the southern port city and home to the British Navy.

The meeting led to the world's top sailors and maxi yachts competing in a race like no other to circumnavigate the globe every four years.

Two years later, the first Whitbread Round the World Race became a reality. The race got underway in The Solent, off the coast of Portsmouth, in early September. Seventeen yachts of various sizes and rigs took part. Famed ocean adventurer Chay Blyth skippered Great Britain II. The Mexican yacht Sayula II won the overall race in 133 days and 13 hours.

In September 1989, twenty-three, multi-class boats left the starting line in Southampton for the 33,000 nautical mile race. With the handicap system scrapped, the competition was divided into four divisions. The race made history with the first all-female crew competing on board Maiden, skippered by the boat's owner Tracy Edwards.

One day in late November, I decided to take a stroll down to Fremantle Sailing Club to see if any of the Whitbread boats were in the harbour, having navigated the 7,260 nautical mile second leg from Puerto Punta del Este in the Maldonado Department of eastern Uruguay.

I always enjoyed my time down by the sea in Freo, soothed by the warm winds that floated off the Indian Ocean in summer and the tintinnabulation of the chimes gently dancing from the boat masts.

By some distance and time, the New Zealand boat Steinlager II had been the first in the fleet to arrive in Fremantle on November 2, having spent 27 days, two hours, and thirty-four minutes at sea. The last of the boats arrived on December 7. The fleet was in Freo up to two days before Christmas when they set off on the third leg to Auckland.

That morning in the yacht club, I was hoping to meet up with some of the 16-member crew from the Sail Ireland entry, NCB, led by Corkman Joe English - the 'People's Skipper'. Reports had appeared in the Irish media about NCB which were far from sanguine about the boat's prospects in the Whitbread. It resulted in the initials forming a less kind moniker for the boat – 'Never Coming Back'.

While there was so sign of any of the boat's crew in or around the club, I was surprised to spot someone that I'd known from my magazine days back in Dublin. The man was his usual effervescent self, busily chatting to a group of other sailors sitting in the members' lounge.

It was none other than the unflinching Enda O'Coineen, seafarer extraordinaire and founder of *Afloat* magazine. The Galwayman had previously crossed 2,800 nautical miles in the North Atlantic single-handedly in a sixteen-foot rubber dinghy. He described the conditions as "seas in which rocks would float". For Enda, anything safe was a holiday. The ocean was the axis around which his life turned from when he was a young boy.

In 1977, at the age of 21, Enda made his first attempt at crossing the Atlantic in a rib, setting out from Boston Massachusetts, only to be capsized a few hundred miles short of Ireland. He was scooped out of the sea by the British Navy. Enda thanked the captain for his kindness. However, the lure of the waves was too much. He politely asked to be put back into the ocean aboard his now-righted vessel so that he could continue with his voyage. His request was refused.

Eight years later, in 1985, after logging up many further ocean-miles, he resumed his unfinished business with the North Atlantic. Kilcullen III was scarcely more sophisticated than Kilcullen I. Nor was the lone sailor one whit less antsy the second time round, in the face of "shoreside doubters" and the threats posed by icebergs, sharks, whales and the constant cold and wet. Not to mention his own, understandable questioning mindset.

In the end, Enda made it home safely. He staggered ashore near Waterford at dead of night. He let himself into a small hotel and fell asleep on the first unoccupied bed he found. Little did he know at the time that the local press corps had a search party out for him as they wanted to interview him.

As he wrote in the foreword to his book, *The Unsinkable Kilcullen – Across the Atlantic by Inflatable and Other Ways to Get Wet*, Enda was always adventurous "and, at times, considered wild". He had heard himself being described as "an uncontrolled missile going through life". Others labelled him "the ultimate survivor".

I ask myself, what is it that prompts someone to sail single-handedly in small boats across oceans? And what happens to them when they succeed – or fail? The cast of solo sailors comprises a certain type of person - eccentric, driven, flamboyant and brave.

Richard King, author of *Sailing Alone: A History*, wrote "a solo voyage across an ocean alone for anyone has a significant, even primary aspect of social and artistic performance".

"Man, Overboard Portside!"

Robert Manry, a copy editor from Ohio who crossed the Atlantic in a 13.5-foot boat in 1965, alluded to this when he said he wanted to craft his voyage "into something nearer to a work of art than my life on land has been".

Aware that day in Fremantle that Enda wasn't part of the NCB crew, I greeted him with a firm arm around the shoulder and the query: "What the hell are *you* doing here?" As was his nature, he responded with a sardonic quip. "I've been sailing halfway around the world, what have you been up to recently?" We reminisced and joked over coffee and sandwiches.

Enda informed me that he was crewing on board a 22-metre British maxi called With Integrity. The former Great Britain II was the veteran of the fleet, having completed all four previous Whitbreads. The maxi sloop was heavier than the new maxi's division and she raced in the Cruiser class. He then began to tell me all about the heart-stopping experiences he and his fellow crew members encountered on the race's second leg from Punta del Este. At the time of the incident, they were sailing around the Cape of Good Hope, just off the coast of South Africa.

It is located at the southern tip of the Cape Peninsula and about 50 kilometres to the north of Cape Town, the legislative capital of South Africa. It was originally named the Cape of Storms in the 1480s by Portuguese explorer Bartolomeu Dias. John II of Portugal renamed it the Cape of Good Hope as its discovery was a good omen that India could be reached by sea from Europe.

The channel near the Cape, where the Atlantic and Indian oceans meet, can be treacherous for cargo ships, never mind ocean-going racing boats made of fibre glass. The warm Agulhas current from the east runs into the cold Benguela current from the northwest. Dangerous waves from these ocean streams have caused serious accidents. The coastal line is marred with almost 3,000 sunken vessels, earning the Cape the alias the 'Graveyard of Ships'.

With Integrity was crashing through the waves around the Cape when a sailor was suddenly swept overboard. Fortunately, several other crew members were on deck to witness the unfortunate accident. Ocean racing yachts move through the waves at a frantic pace of nautical knots, and it requires skill and composure to turn a maxi around in double quick time.

From South Africa, Antarctica is the next land mass to the south – the world's coldest, highest, windiest continent. The average sea temperature around the Cape in November is sixty-three degrees Fahrenheit, or just over seventeen degrees Celsius - roughly the same as the highest temperatures in the Irish Sea in late summer, early autumn.

While the sea temperature was reassuring in terms of providing 'good hope' for a person's safe rescue, the local currents and mountainous waves swirling nearby were a constant reminder of the peril. A person would need all their physical and mental resources, not to mention a generous dollop of luck, to survive in such conditions.

"Man, Overboard Portside!"

Enda reckoned that they were able to turn the boat around in under twenty minutes. They then needed to return to the stretch of sea where the accident occurred and try and locate the missing sailor. It was a daunting task.

Fortunately, nature came to his aid, in the shape of the world's largest flying bird by wingspan. As With Integrity sped back through the waves to where the sailor fell overboard, members of the crew saw something overhead. It was a wreck of albatrosses, each with a wingspan of 3.6 metres. What caught the birds' attention was an object they saw floating in the sea below, which they thought was food.

Enda takes up the story...

"Accidents happen when you least expect. It was a very cold day in bright sunshine dancing off the wave tops. It was morning time. We were moving with one reef in main under full spinnaker at speed.
We went down a big wave, the spinnaker slacked. Our crewman, Willie, raced deck with only tracksuit and sea boots. As we came up, the wave spinnaker line hardened and picked him up over the side in an instant.
I saw him slide past, staring helplessly up and being whisked away. He had the remarkable presence of mind to remove his wellies and trap the air in them upside-down and keep his head above water. I never thought I'd see the day when a simple pair of wellies would save a mate's life. Some of the giant albatrosses following us broke away. An early lunch? They hovered over his head. So, on slashing the spinnaker lines away and an expensive sail list, we rapidly turned and pointed the boat at the albatross.
It was highly emotional. It all happened so fast. Willie was lucky to be alive."

Long live albatross! Ironically, when it comes to put-downs, the albatross is up there. The bird is perceived as being an annoying burden due to the maxim "an albatross around the neck". The adage derives from English poet Samuel Taylor Coleridge's *The Rime of the Ancient Mariner* (1798) where a sailor who shot a friendly albatross was forced to wear its carcass around his neck as punishment.

The albatross considers the Southern Ocean its home as it needs strong winds to make long flights. Tropical seas are often becalmed, which makes them difficult to fly across. On this day, in late 1989, the albatross wreck was the saviour of a sailor grappling for survival in the angry seas off the coast of South Africa.

Willie was pulled back on board, conscious but borderline hyperthermic, which is no surprise given that he was alone in the ocean, in a state of shock, in a race against the clock. Unlike other sailors who went overboard during previous world races, he survived the ordeal.

What's more, hearteningly, he made a full recovery.

In the first Whitbread race in 1973, three sailors were less fortunate and sadly two of them were never seen again. Three men also died tragically during the 1989-'90 race. The British boat Creighton's Naturally suffered a serious broach on the second leg. Crew members Tony Philips and Bart van den Dwey were swept overboard. They were both pulled back on deck. Van den Dwey was resuscitated but after three hours of trying, crew members were unable to revive Philips. A few days later, by radio agreement with relatives ashore, Philips was buried at sea.

Earlier in the race, on the first stopover in Uruguay, there were two tragedies. Fazisi's distraught Russian co-skipper Alexej Grischenko hanged himself in a local park in Punta del Este. Janne Gustaffson from Sweden's The Card was killed in a motorcycle crash in the city a few days later.

There were also a few serious accidents that year. French boat Charles Jourdan collided with a whale on the third leg to Auckland. Finnish entry Martela OF lost its keel and capsized three hundred and fifty nautical miles from the leg four finish. The unharmed crew was picked up from the overturned hull by Charles Jourdan and Merit. Union Bank of Finland also broke off the race to participate in the rescue of its compatriot boat.

The Card lost her mizzenmast after it became entangled with a spectator boat at the start of the fourth leg in Auckland. A maxi, she continued the race as a sloop. The United States hosted the race for the first time at Fort Lauderdale in Florida. Two boats were unable to complete the race and three lost their masts.

A decade before, in August 1979, the Fastnet Race off the coast of Ireland was hit by a freak storm which claimed 19 lives. Ranked as one of the two foremost offshore classics along with the Sydney to Hobart race, the Fastnet, which takes place every two years, attracts entrants from all over the world and has done so since 1925.

Notoriously unforgiving, the event is to nautical what the North Face of the Eiger is to mountaineering. The route is a 695-nautical mile dash from Cowes on the Isle of Wight to the Fastnet Rock, off the coast of Cork, three-and-a-half nautical miles southwest of Cape Clear Island, and back.

The race finishes at the western end of the breakwater in Cherbourg, the port in Normandy in northern France.
It all started at around lunchtime on Saturday, August 11th, 1979, the first day of the race. The BBC Radio shipping forecast predicted south westerly winds, force four to five on the Beaufort scale, increasing to force six to seven for a time. Two days later, winds were reported at force six, with gusts of force seven. The forecast was for winds of force eight.

The leading boat, Kialoa, trailed closely by Condor of Bermuda, was on course to break the Fastnet record set eight years earlier. A large depression, known as 'low Y', formed over the Atlantic Ocean during the weekend. By Monday, it had intensified rapidly and turned northeastwards, reaching about 200 nautical miles southwest of Ireland.

Come Tuesday, the low was centred over Wexford. Land-based weather stations reported gale force winds, with the strongest of them out to sea over the race area. The Met Office assessed the maximum winds as force ten, but many of the sailors believed the winds reached force eleven.

Of the 303 yachts that started the race, 24 were abandoned, of which five had sunk due to high winds and treacherous seas. The rescues could only get underway after 6.30am once the winds had dropped to severe gale force nine. Royal Navy ships, RAF Nimrod jets, helicopters, lifeboats, a Dutch warship and other craft picked up 125 yachtsmen whose boats had been caught in violent storm gusts midway between Land's End and Fastnet. The rescue effort also included tugs, trawlers, and tankers.

"Man, Overboard Portside!"

Fifteen yachtsmen and four spectators died. At least 75 boats capsized and five sank. The adoption of heaving to as a storm tactic proved to be helpful in preventing boats capsizing and turtling during the race. Nonetheless, the disaster resulted in a major rethinking of racing, risks, and prevention.

The handicap winner was the yacht Tenacious, owned and skippered by CNN founder Ted Turner. The winner on elapsed time in the race was the 77-foot SV Condor of Bermuda, skippered by Peter Blake, who went on to win more Whitbread races.

The 1979 Fastnet Race was and still is the deadliest yacht race in history – well ahead of the 1998 Sydney to Hobart race, which left six people dead. The rescue was described as the biggest peacetime life-saving operation in Anglo-Irish history and its impact reverberated throughout the yachting world.

There is a memorial to those who died in the race on Cape Clear Island. Fastnet Lighthouse was automated and converted to unwatched in 1989, ten years after the disaster. In 2011, following a review of aids to navigation, the lighthouse's foghorn signal was silenced permanently.

It was an Irish boatman by the name of Tommy Gibbons who once said that "there is but a plank between a sailor and eternity". Sadly, Tommy, a retired postman, died tragically in an accident in 2009 when he slipped on the pier at Rosmoney, near Westport, in County Mayo.

Returning to the Whitbread race, on May 22nd, 1990, Steinlager II was the first boat to cross the finish line in Southampton. It won every leg in the maxi division. It was the last race in which skipper Peter Blake took part, having competed in the first five Whitbreads and the hapless Fastnet Race in 1979. The first all-female crew on Maiden won two of the three Southern Ocean legs in its division.

It's worth noting that many of the maxi yachts that competed in 1989/90 were almost double the size of the smallest boats in the race, with well over twice the sail area. The net result was that many of the smaller boats finished the longer legs more than ten days after the stage winner. Overall, the last finisher was some 52 days behind Steinlager II's 128-day aggregate time.

The drama on board With Integrity was documented in *The West Australian* newspaper in an interview I did with Enda O'Coineen. A photo of him taken alongside the race boats in Fremantle Sailing Club accompanied the article.
He said there was no comparison between the America's Cup and the Whitbread race. "The America Cup's is showbiz," he claimed unequivocally. "The Whitbread is what ocean racing is all about - it's real sailing for serious, long-distant goers."

Enda's exploits across the world's oceans didn't stop there. Having been involved with the fully crewed Whitbread and Volvo races, he was in awe of the solo round the world sailors, particularly the French competitors and the Vendée Globe single-handed non-stop race.

The Vendée, founded by Philippe Jeantot in 1989, has run every four years since 1992. In 2015, Enda bought himself a sixty-foot Imoca. He trained up and down to the Canary Islands four times and across the Atlantic twice, once solo where he came third in a trans-Atlantic weave. He qualified to be one of thirty sailors to do the Vendée.

After 126 days at sea, the adventure ended abruptly when Kilcullen Voyager's mast broke 180 nautical miles off New Zealand's South Island. Unshrinking, Enda returned to New Zealand where he rebuilt his boat and unofficially completed the Vendée. Kilcullen Souffle du Nord made it into the record books. Enda said he was privileged and honoured to have done it, another tick off his "feck bucket list."

It was a far cry from the early days of solo navigation. Back in 1969, Knox-Johnston relied purely on compass, sextant, speed log and dead-reckoning as he became the first person to sail single-handed, non-stop round the world. No global positioning system (GPS), no autopilot, no internet weather forecasts, and no boat longer than thirty-six feet was eligible to compete.

Chapter 16

Coasting It

"Buy the ticket, take the ride" - Hunter S Thompson

Fremantle, December 1989

The weekend in Perth began early on Friday in the port of Fremantle as we prepared to take a boat trip to Rottnest, a popular island tourist destination. Rottnest lies almost 20 kilometres off the West Australian coast in the Indian Ocean. Surrounded by coral reefs and shipwrecks, the island has 20 bays popular with swimmers, divers, snorkelling enthusiasts.

My good friend Scott Carter felt it was high time he visited 'Rotto' as he'd had never set foot on the 19-square kilometre island in the ten years he'd been living in WA. It was an early Christmas gift to himself.

Rottnest is home to the quokka (*setonix brachyurus*), a rare, short-tailed wallaby the size of a domestic cat. In 1696, Dutch explorer Willem de Vlamingh mistook the animal for a rat – prompting the island's moniker. While small colonies of quokka exist in isolated pockets in WA's south-west, the biggest population resides on Rottnest.

Before we reached the boat terminal, we doused ourselves in high protection sun cream. Scott reminded me that only the state of Queensland had a higher rate of skin cancer *pro rata* in the world. SPF protects against sun damage and is said to reduce the risk of melanoma by fifty per cent.

Sunlight can aggravate skin disorders like acne, rosacea and create excessive levels of melanin in the epidermis top layer of skin. UVA leads to collagen breakdown, which results in fine lines, deep wrinkles, blotchiness, and discoloration. The Aboriginals used mud and leaves to protect themselves against harmful rays. It was long before Franz Greiter invented what became modern-day sunscreen in the 1940s. His thick paste was named Piz Buin after the Alpine Mountain on the border of Austria and Switzerland – a place where sunscreen is a must-have.

Rottnest boasted its own newspaper. The fact that I'd been writing articles for *The Rottnest Islander* provided some useful background and insights for the trip. The island's history dates back 50,000 years, when it was still part of the mainland of Western Australia. Aboriginal artifacts suggest that people lived there until about 7,000 years ago, when rising sea levels cut it off from the landmass.

The island was first known as Wadjemup, which roughly translates as 'the land across the sea where the spirits live.' As with much of Australia's history, Rottnest's past was steeped in tragedy, amid accusations of cultural genocide. Like Alcatraz, the island just off the mainland of San Francisco and Robben Island, off Cape Town in South Africa where Nelson Mandela was incarcerated as 'Prisoner 46664' for 28 years, Rottnest was once a prison.

In 1838, the colonial government set up a prison on the island for Aboriginals, after they had been forcibly removed from their own communities. Records show that around 4,000 Aboriginal men and boys from throughout Western Australia were imprisoned at Rottnest.

Many of the inmates were transported to the island in chains, either over long land distances in sweltering summer heat, or across cold and stormy seas.

The prison itself was cramped and chilly, with up to five inmates in a two-metre by three-metre cell, so everyone had a sleeping width of less than 60 centimetres. Lawbreakers were detained there until 1931, apart from a brief closure between 1849 and 1855. Between 1903 and 1931, the jail also took in prisoners who could not be housed at the dreaded Fremantle Prison on the mainland.

Of the 10,000 convicts sent to Australia from 1850, many of them ended up in Fremantle's maximum-security jail, known as 'The Establishment'. The prison was built by the inmates. They dug tunnels twenty metres deep in search of water. It was the scene of hangings, floggings, daring escapes and riots. The jail was decommissioned in 1991 and became a concert venue.

In more recent times, Rottnest was designated as a class-A nature reserve, with the island's flora and fauna protected by law. Over two centuries of bushfires and clearing stripped much of the island of its vegetation. When combined with limited fresh water and a fragile ecosystem, natural recovery was limited.

However, many walkers and cyclists are impressed by the summer-scented wattle, pine, and tea trees. The Rottnest Island daisy has clusters of tiny, bright blue flowers above tall spikes, while sand dunes are home to beach spinifex, wild rosemary, and sea rocket.

As the island is a car-free zone, tourists get around by bus, on foot or, in our case, by hiring a bike – the most popular mode of transport on Rottnest. From the bike rental shop, we made for Bathurst Lighthouse and on towards the centre of the island. Saltwater lakes occupy ten per cent of the inland space across 200 hectares. The island's twelve lakes include names like Baghdad and Herschel. As it was the height of summer, Pink Lake had completely dried out, leaving swathes of pink pans.

At Serpentine Lake, we spotted a flock of ruddy turnstone. The small wading bird is easily recognised by its short orange legs, distinctive plumage, and tubby shape. It earned its name as it uses its beak to turn over large stones in search of food. The island's salt lakes are home to ninety per cent – or about 500 - of Australia's turnstone population. In April, the bird starts its long flight back to Siberia in time for the breeding season in the Arctic tundra.

The waters in the Rottnest lakes are four times saltier than in the sea, so swimming is not advisable. Yet, remarkably, several plants evolved to cope with the high salt levels. Beaded samphire and coastal pigface were evident close to the lakes' edges, creating a unique wetland habitat. One of the foot trails we trudged up had a boardwalk over the lakes. It created a dreamlike feeling of floating on water.

At Oliver Hill Battery, we inspected the instalment that was part of Western Australia's coastal defence during the Second World War. The site is the only survivor of the seven 9.2-inch coastal gun batteries built during the late 1930s and early 1940s to defend Australia's ports.

During the war, Fremantle was a base for American, British, and Dutch submarines, shipping repairs and acted as a troop convoy assembly point. The Rottnest Fortress, as it was known, complete with underground tunnels, was a deterrent in defending against coastal attacks.

As Scott and I completed a loop around the island, we caught sightings of ospreys, humpback whales and long-nosed fur seals. The pine trees offered refuge from the rippling heat of the midday sun. It gave us our first opportunity us to check out the quokkas up close.

While they are friendly and cute creatures, zoologists point out that quokkas are essentially wild animals that need to be managed to ensure minimal interference in their natural selection. Signs are posted asking tourists not to touch or feed the vegetarian marsupials as their stomachs are unable to digest processed foods. Bins on the island are designed to stop them scavenging food scraps.

The quokkas feed on succulent plants and remain close to freshwater soaks near the salt lakes. To shield them from physical injury and diseases, there are no household pets and foxes allowed on the island. The animal's ability to regenerate damaged muscle tissue has provided links in the understanding of muscular dystrophy in humans.

Feeling hot and slightly bothered, we got back on our bikes and made for the beach. There we enjoyed a swim in the turquoise water. With our throats dry to the bone and our stomachs rumbling, we made for the Rottnest Hotel. The fish 'n' chips and mushy peas we ordered were like manna from heaven, and we made short shrift of a few jugs of ice-cold beer.

We got chatting to a group of English tourists camping under trees near Pinky Beach. They shared a story with us about how a fellow camper called into the authority office to complain about the number of speed boats exceeding the bay's five-knot limit. The marine ranger assured them that every effort was made to stop such lawbreakers, but they had a problem in catching them.

The girls went on a camel ride in Broome. The tour guide told them that there were 200,000 feral camels in Australia, said to be the world's biggest population of Arabian camel. Introduced in the 1840s, they were imported from the Canary Islands to help explore the country's interior – the Nullabor ('no tree'). They are highly mobile animals and can forage over 70 kilometres a day across desert and semi-desert land.

We got back to the jetty at Thomson Bay in time for our twenty-minute return crossing aboard the Star Flyte hi-speed ferry to Fremantle. As Bill Withers' 'Lovely Day' played below deck, we looked out at the choppy sea. The captain welcomed us on board. He said we could expect a bumpy ride.

He wasn't wrong. We bounced about like basketballs. To avoid waves of sea sickness, we kept focusing on the horizon. I was lucky, Scott less so. He was adamant that if ever he was to return to Rottnest, he would only fly there by light aircraft.

Chapter 17

Great Scott

"Until what is significant is created by you, you aren't living your life, you are living some inherited life" – Werner Erhard

Fremantle, December 1989

That evening we felt exhausted after our Rottnest adventure and hungry like the wolves. Scott ordered in from Red Rooster on Hamilton Hill. The food arrived in double-quick time, and we gobbled down our roast chicken and chips with relish. "Did you know that smell accounts for as much as 80 per cent of what we taste?" Scott remarked randomly.

I responded to him with a 'is that so?' look. It only encouraged Scott. "Not alone that," he added, "everyone has up to 10,000 taste buds, most of them on your tongue. The rest are festooned around the inside of your cheeks. Imagine all that action going on in your mouth... "Can I interest you in a glass of chardonnay, Mike?" Scott said. "*Por favor!*" I replied, not knowing if he understood Spanish, let alone the unintentional pun.

Scott had a strict but happy childhood. His mother, Juliette, was born in Paris. His father, Edward, a phlegmatic character, was a British diplomat. His career took the family to four countries on three continents over 25 years. Scott grew a curiosity about the world. He had a love of travel from which he gathered endless stories.

The Carters never settled anywhere they called home until they arrived in Australia in 1974. Ed worked at the British Embassy in Canberra, until he retired in 1979. The family then moved to WA. His father's hobby was collecting works of art. Hanging in Scott's living room was a print of 'Impression, Sunrise' which Claude Monet painted at Le Havre, in northern France, in 1872. His father urged him to treasure the painting not just for its mesmeric beauty but because it marked the birth of modern art and the christening of Impressionism.

Before the Carters arrived in Australia, they lived in India. Scott enjoyed his days in Delhi, particularly his morning strolls through the city's Lodhi Gardens. There he would marvel at the tombs' Indo-Islamic architecture, resting places for several 15th century rulers from the Lodhi dynasty.

Some days he might walk over by Humayun's Tomb. Built in the 1560's, it was the first garden mausoleum on the Indian subcontinent and in whose cells are buried over 150 family members from the Mughal empire.

It was during his time in Delhi that Scott took up yoga. He subscribed to a yogi who boasted that his savasana corpse pose had the power to cure stress and anxiety. The guru claimed the extent of his talents made him "a catalyst for world peace".

It wasn't long before the man was exposed as a charlatan, a magnet for money and influence. He tried to convince his clients that he could make each one of them a *crorepati* (millionaire), while trying to line his own pockets. The business went bust and its founder was jailed for fraud.

Our conversation moved to Canberra, Australia's federal capital. I was keen to know if Scott liked living there as I'd heard conflicting reports about the place. My prime interest was sparked by the fact that I'd recently applied for a job as a press officer with the Department of Education and was waiting on word back.

I asked Scott if my life would be any the poorer if I wasn't hired. "Certainly not," he said. "Canberra can't compare to Perth - unless, of course, you the type of person who finds the company of bureaucrats stimulating." I didn't get the job. Nor did I ever get a chance to visit the city.

It was a typical summer's night in Freo, still, pleasantly warm, and with a clear sky. Scott loaded up the esky with XXXX stubbies and ice and we moved out to the garden. Washing hung on the rotary line, bone dry and stiff from the sun. A kookaburra's chuckle vied with the chirrups of the crickets.

I stretched out on a leather couch, so old and decrepit it could have accommodated Captain Cook and his crew on the Endeavour as they sailed into Botany Bay in 1770. I was dying to slip my hands all the way down the sides of the sofa in the hope of finding something precious.

"Wrap your laughing gear 'round that," Scott said handing me a beer. "You'll need this too," he added as he reached for a can of No Bites insect repellent. "We've heaps of mozzies. They breed in the swamp up the way in Spearwood. Oh, and lay off the after-sun mate, they love the bloody stuff."

Being tormented by mosquitoes is something I knew a little about from my days living in Katherine. One evening, after hosing the back garden wearing only a pair of shorts, my back was covered in bites. When I awoke the next day, I felt as weak as a bled calf. The doctor told me that I had contacted Ross River virus, and the symptoms were fever, rash, and joint pain. It took a few days for the torpor to abate.

As twilight faded, we marvelled at the expanse of a star-filled firmament and crescent moon. Scott looked up from his director's chair. "That's out of this world," he said with no sense of irony. "You know mate, mention the Milky Way to any kid today and they'd say to you 'chocolate bar'. Rather unfortunate, don't you agree?"

He nattered on about the stellar wonder above us, the Southern Cross. In the background, Leonard Cohen waxed lyrical about ringing the bells that still can ring. Cohen's words urged us to take the conversation to a higher plateau. "Do you like poetry?" he asked. "Can't say I do," I replied with a lack of certainty. He said I should give it a go. My life would be enriched. "Ever heard of a Welsh poet by the name of WH Davies? No, never, I confirmed.

"Davies was a gifted poet who spent much of his life as a hobo," he said. "There's a line from one of his poems, entitled *Leisure*, which goes: '*What is this life if, full of care/ We have no time to stand and stare? / No time to see, in broad daylight/ streams full of stars, like skies at night*'. Nice one, yeah?"

I suggested to Scott that he should check out the works of Ireland's most noted poets – WB Yeats, Patrick Kavanagh, Seamus Heaney. He said that he had started – not once, but countless times - to read James Joyce's *Ulysses*, but he couldn't make sense of it. About a third way through the 18 chapters, he gave up. He was in good company.

A dog joined us in the garden. "I never knew you had a pet," I said. "I don't," Scott replied. "That's Arnie, my sister Kate's mutt. I'm minding him while she's in Sydney for a job interview. He's a short-haired dachshund – a house dog. He sleeps in the spare room. Every morning and in the evening when it's cool, he goes outside for a pee. I've quite taken to him. He's perky."

Scott liked dogs, that was obvious, but he'd no time for cats. "Guess what," he said, "roaming pet cats kill over 500 million animals a year in Australia - about 300 million of which are native animals." "Get out of it!" I replied. "True. And not only that," he added, "studies show that hunting pet cats kill 30 to 50 times more native animals per square kilometre in suburbs because of their high numbers than feral cats kill per square kilometre in the bush." "Huh, that's something," I responded crisply.

Scott was in a chipper mood. He asked me if I sailed. I told him that I enjoyed time on the water, but I'd never call myself a sailor. He pointed to the hull of a boat lying opposite him in the garden. He told me that if I ever wanted to join him for a jaunt on the Swan River to give him a shout. Judging by the dinghy's sorry state, it was some time since he and 'Salacia' had spent an afternoon together on the water.

He then returned to talking about India. With his round spectacles perched on the bridge of his aquiline nose, he waxed lyrical about the country's architecture and his favourite building - the Tomb of I'timad-ud-Daulah in the city of Agra in Uttar Pradesh. Scott qualified as a solicitor specialising in corporate law, but architecture had been his first career choice.

The Indian subcontinent boasts some of the world's finest architectural and archaeological treasures. 'Baby Taj' with its hand-painted walls was the draft for the more famous Taj Mahal, the ivory-white marble mausoleum also known as the Crown of the Palace.

Its build was commissioned in 1631 on the order of Mughal emperor Shah Jahan as the burial ground for his favourite wife, Mumtaz Mahal. Princess Di was photographed sitting alone at the front of the Taj in early 1992, the year she and Prince Charles split up.

Scott knew a lot about India's history. He told me that several Irish people played key roles in India's colonial administration, reflecting Ireland's complex relationship with empire. By 1860, one third of the men running British India were Irish. Tipperary man Michael Dwyer governed Punjab at the time of the Amritsar Massacre.

The slaughter in Amritsar occurred on April 13th, 1919. British Indian Army officer Colonel Reginald Dyer, who was educated in Midleton, County Cork, and studied medicine at the Royal College of Surgeons in Dublin, gave the order for his soldiers to open fire at a demonstration which resulted in the deaths of at least 379 unarmed protesters.

Dwyer staunchly defended Dyer's actions. It earned Dyer the tag the 'Butcher of Amritsar'. India learned how the Irish rebelled against British rule – from ideology to the tactics of freedom fighting. It was a phenomenon repeated across the colonial world. Having helped to build the empire, Ireland then sought to dismantle it.

Scott returned to India umpteen times on business trips. He visited Calcutta, the country's cultural centre, which boasts the highest number of Nobel laureates in the sprawling country. Corporate law has been a fixture in the city since the trading days of the British East India Company.

During the company's exploitative rule, 'mayor's courts' resolved settlements between traders dealing in cotton and spices. India's Supreme Court has been based in New Delhi since 1950, soon after the country left the British Empire. However, Calcutta remained a centre of corporate law.

Scott was impressed by the city's bankruptcy court with its high ceilings, ornate plasterwork and a portrait of India's most famous lawyer, Mahatma Gandhi. However, the abject poverty in Calcutta devastated him, not least the many authorised and unauthorised slums. The city's population has trebled from under five million in 1950 to 15 million today. In 2011, Calcutta was renamed Kolkata.

On Scott's sideboard lay his most precious keepsake – a shiva lingam stone, brownish with beige touches woven through it. Part of the quartz family, the lingam stone is found in only one of seven sacred rivers in India. He once saw villagers on the banks of the Narmada River, which flows through the states of Madhya Pradesh and Gujarat, polishing the rocks into a lingam shape.

The stones range in size from a chicken's egg to forms as tall as ten feet. In Hindu culture, shiva means 'sign' or 'symbol'. The lingam represents a cosmic egg, stabilising male, and female energies. It raises aspects of fertility, sexuality, and confidence. The stone's rounded ends are said to increase memory and consciousness. The larger lingam enhances intimacy. It is placed as a totem in a bedroom to promote sacral chakra and create a healthy balance in mind and body.

As the hours slipped away, bouts of silence stretched out. We took turns in sounding off about the meaning of life. Philosophies were shared on how we might make the world less unforgiving. "They say travel helps people become more caring," Scott remarked. "A migrating swift will see more of the world in a year than most of us will in our entire lives, soaring above deserts, jungles, and savannahs. They must be highly empathetic."

As swifts zip through the skies on their long, thin wings, they feed on tiny airborne creatures, spiders, and small insects. They bathe by flying through rain showers; they mate in flight; they sleep on the wing, and unlike most migrating birds, which often rest and feed, swifts will hurtle through the skies for months. The only time these birds land is to nest. "Perhaps we should all sprout wings and take off," I opined.

Scott had a glimmering brain with an IQ of 130. A self-effacing gentleman, ill-used by life. He chose to hide his light. For him, anonymity was a badge of honour.

While he wasn't bashful, he would have felt out of place swanning about Perth's gilded circles. He tended to kick difficult decisions and challenges that appealed for action to touch. He was open to the truth in every sense, despite what he thought he might know. His personality was enriched by his education. During the four years he lived in Ireland, he attended the Quaker-run Newtown School in Waterford. It may explain his modest view of his own importance and the weight of his opinion.

Such humility meant he never tried to force his opinions on others or lord over with his intelligence. He was quick-witted and unconsciously funny. He delivered corny jokes as ably as any wannabe stand-up: "Mike, did you know that Australian prime ministers don't speak French? Such is life!" My smile dimmed a fraction, then brightened.

Scott was a Spike Milligan fan. They both spent time in India, Milligan in Rangoon. In an interview with Michael Parkinson on the BBC, Milligan was asked if it was true that his father told him that he killed an elephant with his bare hands. "Well, son," his dad said, "would you rather have an exciting lie, or a boring truth?" The former Goon loved Australia but would only travel there by boat: "Flying isn't dangerous, crashing is."

Whenever Scott and I met we talked at length about lots of things, but politics was regarded as out of bounds; there's enough bloodshed in the world. He saw politicians as an unsavoury bunch of dimwits. "They warp the integrity of society by being unaware of anything that doesn't serve their interests," he remarked - "and, unlike our heroic swifts - they're devoid of empathy."

When it came to elections, Scott always voted – it's against the law not to in Australia. Inevitably, he backed the Liberal Party candidate on the ticket as he favoured keeping Australia in the Commonwealth. In his kitchen, high up in a glass cabinet reserved for nicknacks, a pair of Wedgwood china mugs commemorating the 1953 coronation of Queen Elizabeth II, had pride of place. When making tea, he referred to the Lipton brew as "a cuppa char".

Scott was aware that politically I was more inclined towards the Australian Labor Party, if only for the contingents of Irishmen who campaigned for better working conditions on Fremantle's wharfs. However, that evening under the stars we felt playful, so we decided to amuse ourselves by recounting the mischievous rants of Labor's Paul Keating.

As political leaders go, Keating was Marmite – or rather Vegemite. Depending on your prejudice, the boiler-maker's son from the disadvantaged Sydney suburb of Bankstown was either a colourful firebrand, whose turn of phrase and fearless style of rhetorical jousting perked up Australian politics no end, or someone who was defined by his arrogance and a proclivity for profane abuse.

The *Guardian* accused Keating of climbing the rungs of the Labor Party through political mastery, deftness and "a volcano of verbal bastardry that erupted from his mouth like perpetual lava". No one was spared his snarky comments, and he had the defiant look of a schoolyard bully.

Keating once accused party colleague Jim McClelland of "having swallowed a fucking dictionary". He even referred to the man who was his inspiration and whom he later deposed as party leader, Bob Hawke, as 'Old Jellyback'. When Hawke proposed an over-generous tax concession to sport, Keating threatened to stick to him "like shit to a blanket".

In 1992, as prime minister, Keating famously first introduced the idea of mandatory detention for 'unlawful arrivals' into Australia. He saw to it that the tiny tropical island of Nauru in the Pacific Ocean became synonymous with asylum seekers and refugees trying to enter the country. Even staunch critics admitted that his economic policies helped Australia withstand the global shocks that shattered other more powerful countries.

Keating's most potent vitriol was saved for his Liberal opponents. In 1993, when he was asked by Liberal leader John Hewson why he wouldn't call an early election, he lambasted him: "Mate, because I want to do you slowly. And in the battle stakes we're stripped down and ready to go." He labelled Hewson "a feral abacus" whose performance was "like being flogged by warm lettuce... or being mauled by a dead sheep".

In 1994, he let rip at his opposite number, Andrew Peacock, saying he should be "put down like a faithful old dog" and that the "poor old thing" was more to be pitied than despised. A year later in parliament, he asked the speaker to give John Howard a Valium tablet as he was "wound up like a thousand-day clock... one more half turn and there'll be springs and sprockets all over the building."

Keating described Howard as "a little desiccated coconut" and said his Liberal Party "couldn't raffle a duck in a pub". Scott found the barbs amusing. We ignored discussing Keating's fervent view that Australia's ambition should be to exit the Commonwealth "as soon as possible". While he had nothing against the British monarchy *per se*, the immutable fact was that her royal highness was on the other side of the world and however conscientiously and ably she performed the role of Australian head of state, she could never symbolise or express "our Australianness".

Scott then asked me how my recent interview with the State Premier of Western Australia, Peter Dowding, had gone. "There's not much to tell you, really," I replied in the hope we might digress from discussing politics. It was not to be. Dowding's press officer afforded me a 20-minute interview on the drive from his office to Parliament House, I said.

Not only was the time extremely tight, but the premier was a barrister. Interviewing a legal eagle can be like throwing pebbles into Niagara Falls. I asked him about the State's finances and the more complex matter of his relationship with his immediate predecessor, Brian Burke.

In 1988, Burke became Australia's ambassador to Ireland and the Vatican, living in the 'Abbey Lea' consular residence in Killiney, in south Dublin. He had to revoke both of his roles in 1991 and was ordered to appear before the WA Inc Royal Commission. The body examined the political scandal surrounding dealings with prominent businessmen, including Alan Bond, Laurie Connell, and Warren Anderson. The dealings resulted in a loss of public money of at least $600 million and the closure of several large corporations.

Burke was not found criminally responsible for anything to do with WA Inc. The commission ruled that he had falsely claimed $17,000 from a parliamentary travel account between 1984 and 1986. In July 1994, Burke, a former journalist with *The West Australian* and TV reporter, and a devout Catholic, was sentenced to two years in prison. He was released on parole after seven months.

In 1995, he was stripped of his Order of Australia honour. Two years later, he was found guilty of stealing $122,585 in campaign donations to the Labor Party. He was sentenced to three years jail but was released after six months, when his conviction was quashed on appeal. Dowding was circumspect in his response, it was unlikely that himself and Burke were bosom pals. He simply said that 'Burkie' was the ambassador in Ireland, while his job as premier was to lead the State government.

We'd had enough of politics, so I pressed Scott on his job. He was cagey at first, but soon relented. "Corporate law is so bloody boring," he said. "In my job, it's a matter of professional pride to be dull." Relations between himself and his boss had sundered. He described him as an angry man who could "cut hedges with his tongue". Wearily rubbing his eyes, he pressed two fingers against the bridge of his nose. He knew that he faced a crossroads in his life.

Scott was in the mood for talking now. From what he said about his ex-partner, Roz, she seemed like a free spirit. I pictured a mistress of boho chic with a bandana and flowers in her hair. Tom Hanks' beloved Jenny (Robin Wright) in *Forrest Gump* sprung to mind. Scott and Roz were together for seven years, during which time they had a son named Barry.

After they split up, 'Bazza' went to live with his mother near the beach front at Scarborough, in north Perth. Father and son kept in touch and saw each other regularly. Scott was fond of being on his own, "doing his own thing", as he put it. He proffered a heartfelt quote from *Shirley Valentine*: "Marriage is like the Middle East, isn't it? There's no solution."

The magic of the night endured. We downed beers with abandon, oblivious to the countless times we visited the dunny (outside loo). Here we were, two youngish men in our prime, healthy, and happy, and on the cusp of yet unexplored journeys. The way to go.

Joy for Scott was measured by how carefree his future would prove. Before he took up law, he worked on a trawler fishing for cray out of the port of Exmouth, in the seas off Western Australia's Northwest Cape. The pay was good, but the work was exhausting and the living conditions squalid.

Crew members were on duty for months on end and went weeks without a day off. Apart from the hardship, the work was fraught with danger. Serious accidents involving winches during hauls were not unusual. Despite everything, Scott imagined how his life might have turned out had he chosen to stay on at sea.

Shifting course again, he asked me if I'd noticed a certain building on the approach road to Fremantle. It was painted a greyish colour, and all its windows were shuttered. Above the front door was a neon sign that flashed with the name 'Harem' in red letters. Was old-school Scott now about to share a secret? To lay bare that he had visited a brothel.

He proceeded with his story. At the building's entrance, he nervously pressed the buzzer. On hearing a voice, he gently pushed open the door. A small, middle-aged woman stood before him. "She was the person in charge," Scott said. "You mean madam," I replied, in a minor act of cruelty. She introduced him to the five escorts seated on red leather couches in a dimly lit hallway.

Scott pointed at one of the girls. "Belle," he said coyly. It was the only name he could remember. The tall brunette took him by the hand. They walked past scented candles resting on tables covered in sheets of white paper. As they entered a small box room, Belle read out the prices while clinically removing a condom from its sachet. She asked Scott if he had preferences.

Inside, he shuddered. He asked her for a 'three-legged dog' and handed her a wad of notes. Belle stood beside the bed. She had her back against the wall and Scott faced her. He lifted one of her legs and wrapped it around his hip - as if the two of them had three legs. The raw thrill was too much. The passion that he had long yearned had dissipated.

Embarrassed, he turned and looked at his watch. Belle straightened the straps on her negligee and brushed her hair back behind her shoulders. Feeling short-changed but too bashful to react, Scott left the brothel through the back door. He poked his head out above the step and checked the darkened street to make sure the coast was clear. He trundled home, his ego deflated and his wallet eighty dollars the lighter.

Was his visit to Harem an act of impulse? Had he indulged in other sexual peccadilloes? "It wasn't my first time to visit a knocking shop Mike, if that's what you're asking," he replied with mild indignance. "And you know what, I've no qualms about paying for sex – none, *nada*," he added, with uncharacteristic vigour.

I was surprised by Scott's candour. Not by his honesty - he was always frank – but by his willingness to share his past exploits generously.

He told me that his pursuit of casual sex began in his late teens, while he was working in a bar in Kalgoorlie. The West Australian town, situated almost 600 kilometres north-east of Perth, was known far and wide for gold mining - and prostitution.

In 1892, an event near Coolgardie sparked the largest gold rush in WA's history which resulted in a mass migration of people to the area. A year later, there was a second discovery of gold in a town called Hannan, later renamed Kalgoorlie. Within three days of the find by prospector Patrick Hannan, another 700 men arrived to try their luck.

What was a one-horse town up to less than a decade before, saw its population jump to 2,018 within six years. While most of the increase was down to the number of panhandlers, a large proportion was explained by an influx of prostitutes. In fact, while the number of men in Kalgoorlie doubled by 1903 to 3,904, the female population increased almost six-fold to 2,886 in less than five years.

Gold rush stations were often isolated communities of mainly men. At the time, prostitution was an accepted part of establishing law and order, and for whatever reason it was seen as a sort of safety valve in the face of widespread alcohol abuse and violence. Kalgoorlie earned itself a reputation as a wild-west town, known for its three Gs – gold, girls, and grog.

More recently, some of the town's 30,000 residents were able to trace their family history to the brothels as working women settled down to raise a family. With the passing of years, demand for the local brothels flagged. Men willing to pay for sex and porn services turned their attention to internet sites and mobile phones.

One woman arrived at a local brothel at the age of 44. She was unskilled and had fled physical abuse elsewhere. The safety offered by a legitimate working house and the money she made meant that 14 years later, she owned three houses, mortgage-free. The brothel's madam is said to have passed the woman off to clients as being eleven years younger by dimming the lights.

Scott asked me what the scariest experience in my life was.

Was there ever a moment when I was convinced the game was up? I told him about the time I flew from Perth to Colombo in Sri Lanka. Half-way through the 11-hour flight, while cruising at a height of 10,000 metres above the Indian Ocean, the plane hit an air pocket, and suddenly lost altitude. I was beyond petrified. Numb to the bone.

Needs must at a time of such a mortal threat. Although I exercise my faith in God with discretion, it was an instant for Hail Marys and making pleas to any higher powers that may have cared to listen. Fortunately, no one on the flight that day was injured. Apparently, such incidents, when planes suddenly encounter air pockets occur from time to time in that part of the world, with reports of flight attendants losing their lives in appalling circumstances.

I then recalled an equally discomforting incident from my early twenties. In this case, I didn't recognise the danger I was in at the time. The incident took place while I was on a holiday in Spain. My friend, AJ Fagan, and I were in a pub one night, chatting up two girls at the bar.

Later, we offered to walk them back to their apartment. When we got to the reception, we found the lift was out of order. We went to the emergency exit door and climbed the steps at the side of the building. When we reached the third or fourth floor, we chatted and joked for a while before saying goodnight. AJ and I returned to the ground floor only to find the main door to the building locked.

We decided it might be best to head back up the stairs and knock on the door of what we assumed was the girls' apartment. No answer. We decided it might be best not to knock again as we weren't sure we were in the right place – or even on the right floor. In a moment of recklessness, I suggested we throw caution to the wind and jump from the window ledge.

Fortunately, my friend was less hasty.

AJ took a coin from his pocket and gently tossed it out into the dark. "Wait a sec, Mick," he quietly insisted, "listen..." After what seemed like an age, the sound of metal could be heard gently striking the ground. The alarm was clear as a bell. I remain ever grateful to AJ – my guardian angel - for having my back that night.

Scott was a voracious reader and always had his head in a book. He enjoyed sharing insights from what he read. He asked me if I was familiar with novels by American writer Armistead Maupin. "You know something Mike," he said enthusiastically, "Maupin's *More Tales of the City* is one of the finest books I've ever read. He's a man who has spent his life campaigning for gay rights... And Bazza is gay, so his writings were of interest to me."

Maupin came up with the maxim of Mona's Law, which says you can have "a hot job, a hot lover and a hot apartment", but you can't have all three at the same time. Everyone must distinguish between wants and needs in life. It got me thinking, I still had a lot of choices to make.

It was now almost 3am, and we'd been chatting for over six hours. After sharing our stories and tales of the unexpected, we felt tired and invigorated at the same time. At the close of a memorable night, Scott and his erstwhile pet made their way upstairs.

I was happy to kip down on the old garden sofa. The sweetest of dreams could never hold a candle to that night under the stars in Freo. It felt as though the Aboriginal ancestors, who returned up high after creating the earth, had looked down at us and wished us well.

Chapter 18

Gutsy Pom

"If your ship doesn't come in, swim out to meet it!" – Jonathan Winters

Fremantle, February 1990

Perth is a picturesque and well-planned city. It boasts a host of top-class restaurants and bars. Without question, from all the fine dining eateries in the central business district (CBD) my personal favourite was The Mediterranean.

Located in the suburb of Subiaco, The Med, as it was known to regular patrons, was bought in 1989 by one of Australia's most famous business tycoons, Alan Bond. He paid former Rothwells merchant banker Laurie Connell $2 million for the property. In 1996, at the age of 49, Connell famously spent the last weekend of his life playing on the losing side in a country polo game and umpiring another. The next day, he had a heart attack at his wife's mansion.

It was not so much the quality of the cuisine that made The Mediterranean special. It was more the garden restaurant's ambience – lush, luxurious, and topped with a cosy, easy-going atmosphere. Like Michel Roux's Le Gavroche in London and The Unicorn in Dublin, the eatery became a favourite haunt of Perth's movers and shakers in the 1980s. It was *the* place to be seen at lunchtime on a Friday.

The Med was run by Bond's first wife, Eileen. She was known as Red, because of her striking hair colour. A formidable woman, always the life of a party.

'Bondy' married Eileen Hughes in 1955. She was from a prominent, well-connected Catholic family in Fremantle. She was a cousin of John Hughes, a high-profile Perth car dealer who advertised heavily in local media.

They were both seventeen years old when they married; Eileen was pregnant and still attending convent school at the time. Bond, who had been raised Protestant, converted to Catholicism when the couple wed. Their marriage lasted for 37 years and produced four children - John, Craig, Susanne, and Jody.

Bond was born in the Hammersmith area of London in 1938, the son of a Welsh miner. His family moved to Western Australia in 1950, when he was eleven years old, and they settled in Fremantle. At the age of fourteen, he was arrested and charged with stealing and unlawful trespassing. At eighteen, he admitted planning a robbery after he was found by police roaming the streets of Fremantle dressed in State Electricity Commission overalls and carrying tools.

Bond was flamboyant, larger-than-life. Others labelled him less fondly as a cad. But his supporters waved away his critics as being envious, exponents of the 'tall poppy syndrome' – under-achievers who gloat on 'cutting the heads off' life's heroes. Bond's business interests ranged from brewing to media. He loved sailing and was a serial philanderer.

His work life started in sign writing. His painting of a dingo on the side of a building in North Fremantle became a famous landmark. It is said that the most important requirement for a signwriter is patience.

Painting letters and images outdoors takes time. Endurance too, as standing outside in the sun all day is a stern test of tolerance.

Restraint did not appear to be one of Bond's foremost traits. He was a man in a hurry. His ambitions extended far beyond sign writing. It wasn't long before he got involved in property, developing luxury apartments along the banks of the Swan River. He launched the mighty Bond Corporation.

Bord Corp extended its reach to include brewing, mining, media, and even airships. In 1987, the business took off. Bond bought Australia-wide Channel Nine from media magnate Kerry Packer for $1 billion. In an interview with TV talk show host Andrew Denton, he spoke about the negotiations with Packer. It explained a great deal about how he did business.

"When we first sat down, we said, 'we're either going to sell our stations to you for $400 million, or you're going to sell your stations to us.' Packer said, 'Well, I don't really want to sell my stations.' And I said, 'Oh, is that right?' So, anyway, after much discussion, Kerry thumped the table and said, 'Listen, if you can pay me $1 billion, I'll sell them to you, otherwise bugger off'... Then I rang the National Australia Bank.

"I said, 'Look, I'm in discussions here to buy these television stations. Kerry will sell to me, and what I want to do is put our stations together and then, with Sky Channel, I'm going to float it off as a separate entity and raise the capital to pay for it... Packer said $1 billion was his asking price, but I think I'll get it for $800 million'...

"The bank manager duly rang back and said yes. I said, 'Thank God. I'll go and have some further negotiations with Kerry,' which I did. And true to his word, he never budged one penny off it. So, I settled the deal with $800 million and a $200 million note. He put his own $200 million in. So, I had $1 billion. And we put our other two stations up as collateral, which were worth probably $400 million."

In fact, the agreed price was $1.05 billion. Packer took $800 million in cash and $250 million in subordinated debt. He turned the debt into a 37 per cent equity in Bond Media, which included Channel 9 in Brisbane, and was worth about $500 million. Its value was $1 billion, but it was $500 million in debt. The cricket and polo-loving Packer was quoted as saying: "You only get one Alan Bond in your lifetime, and I've had mine."

1987 was also the year of Australia's first private university, Bond University. After he acquired TQ-9 in Brisbane, Bond settled an outstanding defamation case the radio station had with Queensland State Premier, Joh Bjelke-Peterson, by paying out $400,000.

Bond later said in a TV interview that he paid the money because Sir Joh left him in no doubt that if he was going to continue to do business successfully in Queensland, then he expected the matter "to be resolved".

Also, in 1987, the Bond Centre was established in Hong Kong, located in the Lippo Centre twin tower skyscraper complex. Bond bought Vincent van Gogh's renowned painting Irises for $54 million, a world record fee at the time.

The purchase was funded by a substantial loan from the auctioneer Sotheby's, which Bond failed to repay. Irises was resold in 1990 to the J Paul Getty Museum in Los Angeles.

When not doing business deals, Bond spent his time and money on his hobby - sailing. He became a national hero after he bankrolled Australia's challenges for the America's Cup. In 1978, he was voted Australian of the Year.

Five years later, his Australia II syndicate won the America's Cup, snatching it from the Americans. The New York Yacht Club held the trophy since 1851 – the longest-winning streak in the history of sport. It prompted Australia's prime minister Bob Hawke to make his infamous workplace remark that "any boss who sacks anyone for not turning up today is a bum".

In 1987, during the America's Cup, there was an occasion when Eileen, Bond and his then mistress Diana Bliss, a public relations consultant and theatre producer, all found themselves together – albeit, not by design.

Bliss had travelled to Perth from her home in Sydney and was meeting friends at the Med for lunch, unaware that Eileen and Alan were dining there at the same time. The story goes that an incensed Eileen ordered the restaurant manager to "throw the bitch out". The manager refused, only to watch helplessly as Bliss, seeing her boyfriend arrive, walked over, and greeted him with a kiss. The scene grew fractious when Eileen turned upon a friend of hers who was lunching with Bliss. The drama concluded when the girlfriend, not the wife, was convinced by other diners to leave.

After failing to repay a $194 million personal guarantee on a loan for a nickel-mining project, he was declared bankrupt. He had debts amounting to €1.8 billion. During bankruptcy hearings, he feigned brain damage to avoid questioning – a charade he found unnecessary to maintain afterwards.

In 1989, Bond's first 10-year affair with Bliss ended, though the pair remained friends and later reunited. Still married to Eileen, Bond had taken Bliss to lunch in London where he produced a photo of his latest love, the Perth air hostess-turned-real estate agent, Tracey Tyler. "She's just like you, only younger," Bond remarked.

In 1992, the Bonds got divorced. His lawyers appealed to the media to leave him alone. His physical and mental health crashed. He had open heart operation and was fitted with an aortic valve. He suffered depression and lost the capacity for everyday functions. He found it hard to speak coherently and couldn't cope with simple arithmetic.

Sceptics suggested that the claims were a ruse to delay court proceedings. In 1995, Bond's family bought him out of bankruptcy, with creditors accepting a payment of $12 million, a little over half a cent per dollar. It was the year that Bond married Bliss. The couple attended social events together and frequented Cottesloe Beach.

In 1997, he was sentenced to seven years in prison after he pleaded guilty to using his controlling interest in Bell Resources to deceptively siphon off $1.2 billion into the coffers of the Bond Corp. The funds were used to shore up the group's cash resources, which spectacularly collapsed, leaving Bell Resources in a precarious position.

Greek philosopher Epicurus rated human desires on a spectrum between what he termed necessary desires and corrosive desires. Necessary desires are food, shelter, clothing, and medicine, along with the emotions of friendship and love. Corrosive desires include longings for status, wealth, and power. The wealth required to satisfy a person's necessary desires is limited and easy to get, but the wealth needed to please corrosive desires is unsparing.

Bond was stripped of his 1984 honour as an Officer of the Order of Australia. He was released from Karnet Prison Farm, after serving four years in other minimum-security State prisons. It was a major fall from grace for the man former Labor prime minister Bob Hawke once described as "one of the outstanding exports from Pommyland".

Despite everything and much to her many friends' frustration, Eileen remained loyal to her ex-husband. They could never quite fathom why she chose to ignore the gossip about her husband endlessly fraternising with beautiful, blonde, and considerably younger women.

Bond's final years were afflicted by personal tragedy. His daughter Susanne, a member of the Australian equestrian showjumping team for seven years, died in 2000 from a suspected accidental overdose of prescription medication.

In 2012, Bliss was found dead in the couple's swimming pool. At the time, police issued a statement to say the circumstances of her death were not suspicious. However, it was later confirmed that Bliss, who had battled against depression for many years, had committed suicide. Eileen was on hand to support her former husband.

In the winter of 2015, Alan Bond was again hospitalised. He underwent open-heart surgery in Fiona Stanley private hospital in Perth to replace a valve that had already been replaced 13 years previously. After the operation, he was put on life support in an induced coma.

He died a few days later, on June 15th, aged 77.

Chapter 19

Hollywood Starlet

"Style is a way to say who you are without having to speak" – Rachel Zoe

Perth, February 1990

The publishing company where I worked doubled as a public relations consultancy. From time to time, they found themselves short-staffed. After a meeting one morning, my editor was asked by a PR director if I could possibly help them out with an agency assignment. The client was Unicef, the United Nations' children's charity. My task would be to research background details in preparation for an interview with one of the charity's high-profile goodwill ambassadors.

The person in question was Audrey Hepburn.

While surveying the screen icon's past, I discovered that she visited Ireland in 1964. She was accompanied by her husband, actor Mel Ferrer. She told reporters at Dublin Airport about her plans to spend time with friends, but it was suspected that the real purpose of her visit was the hope she had of finding her long-estranged father.

Her dad, Anthony Hepburn-Ruston, lived on Sydenham Road in Ballsbridge, near Dublin, for over 35 years. Audrey's mother was Dutch noblewoman Baroness van Hemstad. Her father's second wife, Fidelma, was Irish. He died while being cared for in the nearby Baggot Street Hospital at the age of 91. He was buried in Mount Jerome cemetery in Harold's Cross.

Born in Belgium in 1926, Audrey went by the name of Adriaantje when she was young. At the start of the Second World War, the Hepburns moved to the Netherlands to stay safe. Audrey spoke English, Dutch, and French. However, under Nazi occupation, life was tough. She took up ballet but never became a prima ballerina due to the malnutrition she suffered during the war. A weakened childhood left a fingerprint on her physical self.

In 1959, while on location in Mexico filming *The Unforgiven*, the John Huston western starring Burt Lancaster, trouble struck. She fell off a horse and broke her back. She was hospitalised with four broken vertebrae, torn muscles in her lower back and a badly sprained foot. She completed the film by wearing a back brace. Her accident, together with the consumption of such a restricted diet, may have been why she suffered joint strain.

My abiding screen memory of Hepburn was a scene from *Breakfast at Tiffany's* (1961). Her character, the deliciously named Holly Golightly, was feeling gloomy. She pulled out a guitar, settled down on her fire escape and softly sang 'Moon River'. The moment where she lit up a cigarette is one of the most watched smoking scenes in movie history.

It was an odd choice of song for a New York socialite, yet it summed up the public party girl who deep down was a small-town sweetheart with a romantic yearning for a simpler life. Despite her not having any prior experience of singing, Hepburn performed the tune unaided.

Her performance was flawed, yet captive.

'Moon River' was co-written by Johnny Mercer and Henry Mancini. Mercer's inspiration for the song came from his carefree, boyhood days in Savannah, Georgia. During long summer days he and his friends picked huckleberries alongside gently flowing rivers. The references to his "huckleberry friend" was a homage to Mark Twain's Huck Finn.

The song was originally called 'Blue River'. Mercer discovered that the title was already taken, so he changed it. After Paramount Pictures president Barney Balaban watched a preview of *Breakfast at Tiffany's* he ordered that the song be dropped from the film. The normally meek Hepburn told Balaban that it would be over her dead body.

'Moon River' won an Oscar for best original song and scored a double in the 1962 Grammy Awards by winning record and song of the year. More than a million copies of the sheet music were sold in its first print.

She had three miscarriages in her life (1955, 1959 and 1974), one of which resulted from a fall from a horse. Nonetheless, she gave birth to two healthy boys, Sean Ferrer, and Luca Andrea Dotti.

While she once said that "Paris is always a good idea", it was Rome that launched her career. In 1953, she got her first starring role in William Wyler's romcom *Roman Holiday*, playing opposite Gregory Peck. She pipped Elizabeth Taylor at the screen test. Peck demanded that she be given equal billing and that her name should appear in type as large as his. He told the producers: "You've got to change that because she'll be a big star and I'll look like a jerk."

In the movie, she played a princess who takes a break from her European tour in Rome. She fell asleep on a park bench and was found by an American reporter, Peck. When he discovered her regal identity, he tried to get an exclusive interview - but romance intervened. The scene in the film where the couple were riding around the city together on a motorbike resulted in the sale of 100,000 Vespa scooters.

In Stanley Donen's *Charade* (1963), she starred opposite Cary Grant. She wore a Givenchy-designed ski outfit, a chocolate-coloured wool ensemble, worn with matching fur hat, jacket and Ferragamo shoes. It defined her as a woman of exceptional class and panache. Still, to this day, her costume looks modern and graceful.

The week before she was due to visit Perth, our office got a call from Unicef to say that the interview was off.

Sadly, the actress had taken ill. Her medical team told us she was returning to her home in Switzerland.

The next morning, her PA phoned. She said her client had looked forward to doing the interview. Apart from her movies, she intended to talk about her visits to Ireland. She hoped to return to Australia at some stage. I asked her PA to extend my best wishes to her for a full and speedy recovery.

In 1992, George HW Bush, the 41st President of the United States, presented her with the Presidential Medal of Freedom in recognition of her work for Unicef. However, later that year, on her return from a humanitarian trip to Somalia, she was diagnosed with colon cancer.

After undergoing surgery in November, Hepburn died two months later at her home near Lausanne in Switzerland, age 63. American humourist Sam Levenson shared the following verses at her funeral.

Beauty Tips

For attractive lips, speak words of kindness.
For lovely eyes, seek out the good in people.

For a slim figure, share your food with the hungry.

For beautiful hair, let a child run his fingers through it once a day.
For poise, walk with the knowledge that you'll never walk alone.

People even more than things, have to be restored.
Renewed, revived, reclaimed and redeemed and redeemed... Never throw out anybody.

Remember, if you ever need a helping hand,
You'll find it at the end of your arm.
As you grow older you will discover
That you have two hands.

One for helping yourself,
The other for helping others.

The beauty of a woman is not in a facial mole,
But true beauty in a woman is reflected in her soul.
It is the caring that she lovingly gives, the passion that she shows,
And the beauty of a woman with passing years only grows.

As she was laid to rest, the Aga Khan, also a Unicef ambassador, delivered the eulogy. Gregory Peck recited her favourite poem, 'Unending Love' by Indian writer Rabindranath Tagore, part of which read: *"As I stare on and on into the past, in the end you emerge/Clad in the light of a polestar piercing the darkness of time: You become an image of what is remembered forever."*

Hepburn was not the world's finest actress but, as her son Sean said, she was a movie star. Her legacy was further embellished with a host of awards presented posthumously by her friends in Hollywood.

Chapter 20

Home Again

"We live our lives forwards, but we only understand them backwards, after enough time has accrued"
– Duncan Hamilton

Dublin, June 1990

On returning to Ireland after three years away, you notice changes. Some subtle, some more dramatic amid an environment of cautious optimism. Dublin city did not appear to be as drab and dirty as before, but the cost of living in Ireland was still comparatively sky high. Grafton Street shined and the St Stephen's Green Shopping Centre resembled a Louisiana showboat.

Over O'Connell Bridge, old realities lived on as street beggars kept the statues company, squatting on damp cardboard beds in the cold with downcast eyes and outstretched hands. Tourists looked on with disbelief. The country was teeming with chants for the Boys in Green and the new national sport of World Cup football.

House prices were through the roof.

But I was more than pleased to be home again, as new personal and work challenges presented themselves, which I was eagerly looking forward to tackling. Australia was and remains in my heart my second home, but because of its geographical tyranny, it could never be my home-home.

Chapter 21

Helga phones

"Don't wait for permission to be happy" – Maeve Binchy

Dublin, December 1993

A few days before Christmas, two and half years after my return from Australia, Helga phoned me out of the blue to find out how I was getting on and to wish me season's greetings. She was bustling with joy - as upbeat as a cat with two tails. She told me about how her life had changed. How her relationship with Phil had entered a state of flux, and they ended up going their separate ways.

The news of their split came as a surprise to me; it was hard to imagine one without the other. She said that while she still loved and cared deeply for him, she felt that the mutual passion and tenderness they shared, for so long, had vanished. Their laughter was less loud and infectious, their conversations more strained.

Now in her early thirties, Helga had refined her intensions. She longed to start a family. To her dismay, Phil had no interest in parenting. Without wishing to assign blame, she believed that the only sensible course of action left open to her was to follow a new path in life.

When she told Phil that she intended leaving him, he insisted his love for her remained undimmed and begged her to stay. He sat around the house brooding and enmeshed in self-pity.

His depression triggered anhedonia, a condition where someone can't appreciate joy or pleasure. His plight had outpourings of a line from Patrick Kavanagh's poem, *On Raglan Road*: "I love too much and by such and such, is happiness thrown away."

Deep down, Helga suspected that the destruction he experienced as a young boy left an indelible scar, which never fully healed. Such agony was bound to test the emotional bonds in his life, and his mental health. She left him a note, explaining why they could no longer be together. A few months later, Phil quit Katherine. On a whim. He went with the wind.

Helga moved to Melbourne. There she found a city rich in arts and culture, where the weather changed in a flash, offering the prospect of four seasons in one day. Ironically, it was where Phil spent his formative years after he weas orphaned.

The Yarra flows 252 kilometres from Mount Baw Baw Bay to Port Phillip Bay. The Upside-Down River was onomatopoeic as it described its look: once it reaches Melbourne, there's more garbage on the top than there is at the bottom.

Helga worked as a librarian in the suburb of St Kilda. She liked the quietness of the job. She went for walks on the beach and amused herself on the rides at Luna Park. From time to time, she would head off on a weekend yoga retreat. Stress relief came naturally to her; she used a repeated mantra to access a deep, life-giving state of relaxation.

She was now vegan and swapped alcohol and coffee for herbal tea. Her day began with a cocktail of lemon, turmeric, and ginger juice. She listened intently, a reminder that the heart is a muscle. She was spiritual, but not churchy or prayerful. Religions where pledges of unquestioned faith and piety were rewarded with eternal salvation were not for her.

After surveying the faiths on offer, Helga chose Buddhism. What convinced her was the power of karma, how cause and effect impinge on people's lives. She quoted Tibetan Buddhist Pema Chodron: "You are the sky. Everything else... it's just the weather." I could envisage her as a Greenpeace activist, flinging pots of tomato ketchup at famous paintings.

Despite being worldly wise, she was a true Aussie. She epitomised the lyrics of Peter Allen's song 'I Still Call Australia Home'- *"I've been to cities that never close down, From New York to Rio and old London town; But no matter how far or how wide I roam, I still call Australia home."*

Then came Helga's headliner.

"Mike... are you ready for this?" she said. "Ready for *what*," I retorted, sheepishly. "Well..." A beat. "Righty-ho... I met someone. Yeah, and we... hit it off bigtime. I'm married!" The most thoughtful words I could manage were: "Wow! Are you havin 'a laugh?" "Struth!" she cried. "Six months ago, Nick the Greek and yours truly became man and wife. Say g'day to Mrs Diakos! What was I to do, he's adorable. I felt anointed. Our wedding was perfect... I'll send you photos," she said, all a flutter.

Helga Phones

She couldn't resist telling me all about her special day. It began in a registry office. The bride and groom exchanged vows in the presence of family and close friends. They then adjourned to a Greek restaurant and partied with abandon. The bride and groom sashayed on to the dancefloor as Frank Sinatra's 'It Had to Be You' played, charmed by the lyrics *"I wandered around, and I finally found/The somebody who/ Could make me be true"*.

Helga and Nick honeymooned in Vietnam. A shared interest in motorbikes allowed them to explore the hidden gems of the country's roads less travelled. They spent the first few days scooting around traffic and sizzling pans on the sides of Hanoi's streets. With a guide to accompany them, they sped off on their Royal Enfield Himalayan bikes for the lush green countryside, an hour north of the capital.

"It was awesome!" Helga said effusively, "seeing paradise on two wheels. The mountains, the karst rocks. Paddy fields everywhere, with farmers growing rice and tobacco... tea plantations. Thác Bà Lake. The food – especially pho - was to die for and the Vietnamese people are so warm and friendly. Mike, you gotta go there." Yeah, one day, maybe.

After we'd been chatting for about an hour, the faint sound of a baby's cry could be heard. Her other secret was out. She giggled tenderly and told me it was her "babychen", her three-month-old daughter, Kelly - letting her mum know that she was due a feed.

"Go for your life Helga!" I exclaimed, with misty eyes. "You'll be the best mum ever! Parenting is about positivity and hope. That's you, all over."

We began saying our goodbyes, with a promise that one of us would phone again soon. "Love you, take care of yourself," she said wistfully. "You too," I replied, "and remember, living well is the best revenge."

Motherhood was her reward for living an untrammelled life. Before we hung up, I asked her if she'd ever read Robert Fulghum's novel, *All I Really Need to Know I Learned in Kindergarten*. She said no, she hadn't. So, I expanded. Fulghum wrote that we're all a little weird – and life is a little weird. When we find someone, whose weirdness is compatible with ours, we join up with them and fall into mutually satisfying eccentricity and call it love - true love.

The photos she sent me of the newly-weds standing arm-in-arm flashed with life. The bride was the picture of beauty and elegance. A goddess with porcelain skin, sculpted cheekbones, high neckline, and wavy, flowing hair tousled up.

The silken wedding gown she wore was stunning, illuminated by her chandelier earrings. Her diamond signet ring drew attention to her manicured nails painted red. Helga loved to paint the town red – and every other bright shade, too. And the town she now called home was her pot of gold at the end of the rainbow.

Chapter 22

Wrongly Accused

"In a time of universal deceit, telling the truth is a revolutionary act" – George Orwell

Dublin, September 2012

During my time working in the Territory, at around ten o'clock every Monday morning, I'd call into Katherine police station to see if there were any news stories from the weekend. Among the cops with whom I had a good rapport was Sergeant Harry Grimes. Our chats were seasoned with good-natured taunts. "Here's the Irishman!" he'd cry as I sauntered into reception.

The needs of our respective jobs led to an understanding between us – a *quid pro quo*. He was hell-bent on arresting lawbreakers; I sought leads for the next edition. He had a handshake that caused tremors and a temper that would singe off your hair. Harry was at the centre of several major crime stories across the Top End.

It was a Monday morning in September 1988 when we met for coffee. He first asked me if I'd heard about a strange and rather unsavoury incident that occurred at Katherine Hospital over the weekend. I shook my head and reached for my pen and notebook.

Nursing staff discovered a male patient under the bed clothes with an elderly female patient. The man, who lived locally, was in his mid-fifties. He was being treated at the hospital for leprosy and had one leg, one eye, and no fingers. He had alcohol taken and was sexually aroused at the time. I phoned the hospital about the matter later.

There was something else playing on Harry's mind. He wanted to talk to me about the weekend edition of *The Australian* newspaper. They published an update on the Chamberlain case. The long-running story shocked not just every Australian and made headlines across the world. Before filling me in on the latest revelations, he explained his involvement in the case.

He was a uniformed officer stationed at Alice Springs when nine-week-old Azaria Chamberlain went missing at Ayers Rock (later renamed Uluru) in August 1980. The infant's body was never found, and she was presumed dead. At the time of the disappearance, the family were camping in the park near the rock. The parents claimed that a dingo, a wild dog that roams the outback, had taken their baby from the tent. The police launched a major investigation into the incident. The story made headlines worldwide.

A heavily pregnant Lindy Chamberlain was charged and found guilty of first-degree murder. She was imprisoned for three years. Her husband Michael also spent time in jail. As Harry explained, the prosecution case alleged that Lindy had cut Azaria's throat in the front seat of the family car, a 1977 Holden Torana hatchback, before hiding the body in a camera case.

The police alleged that Lindy then joined other campers around a campfire. She fed a tin of baked beans to her son before going to her tent and raising the alarm, crying out that a dingo had taken her baby. The police alleged that she used the time the campers went to search for Azaria to dispose of the body.

"The infant's jumpsuit was our key evidence," Harry said. "The piece of clothing was found a week later about four kilometres from the Chamberlains' tent, with bloodstains on the neck." However, a contentious forensic report found evidence of foetal haemoglobin in stains on the front seat of the family car. Foetal haemoglobin is present in babies six months and younger; Azaria was nine weeks old when she went missing.

Responding to the allegations, Lindy Chamberlain said her daughter wore a matinee jacket over the jumpsuit. There was no sign of the jacket when the child's clothes were found. Questions were put to her as to why the singlet, which was inside the jumpsuit, was inside out. She said she was careful about how she dressed her babies and would never put on a garment inside out.

Her statement conflicted with how the baby's clothes appeared when they were collected by the prosecution as evidence. Harry's gripe was that the Chamberlains had given an assurance that if they were successful in getting a pardon from the Territory authorities, they wouldn't seek compensation. In her defence, eyewitness evidence was presented of dingoes having been seen in the area around the time of Azaria vanished.

Several witnesses took the stand to say they believed fervently the parents' version of events. In a sworn statement, a nurse reported hearing a baby's cry after the time the prosecution had alleged the infant had been murdered.

Evidence was also presented that adult blood also passed the test used for foetal haemoglobin and that other organic compounds could have produced similar results on the test, including mucus from the nose and chocolate milkshakes, both of which were present in the car where Azaria was allegedly murdered.

An engineer by the name of Phil Martin had conducted dingo research for over a decade. He said that contrary to other evidence given in the case, a dingo's shearing teeth can cut right through material as tough as a car seat belt. He also cited an example of a captive female dingo removing a bundle of meat from its wrapping and leaving the paper intact.

The defence case was rejected by the jury. After a further investigation and a second inquest held in Darwin, in October 1982, Lindy was convicted of murder. She was sentenced to life imprisonment. Michael was found guilty as an accessory after the fact and was given an 18-month suspended sentence.

In 1986, the chief minister ordered Lindy's immediate release and the case was reopened following the chance recovery of Azaria's jacket near a dingo lair. A third inquest was held in 1995, which resulted in an open verdict.

It wasn't until September 1988 – after several unsuccessful appeals, including the final High Court appeal - that the Northern Territory Court of Criminal Appeals unanimously overturned all convictions against the Chamberlains. It was the court decision that Harry always dreaded hearing. He felt dejected.

Fresh inquests were opened. In 2012, some 32 years after Azaria's death, the Chamberlains' version of events was officially supported by a coroner. The entire trial process was criticised for being unprofessional and biased. A media 'circus' aroused accusations of sensationalism.

The first of the final hearings in Alice Springs supported the parents' claim and was damning of the police investigation. The findings of the inquest were broadcast live on television - a first in Australia. After Lindy Chamberlain was released and declared innocent, she was paid $1.3 million for false imprisonment. An amended death certificate was issued.

Harry couldn't accept the final verdict. It was impossible for him to believe the innocent plea. It was as if it was a personal slight on his work as a law enforcer. The fact that Lindy Chamberlain was compensated galled him.

The case was seen as one of the greatest miscarriages of justice in Australia's history – and with good reason. The third century Greek philosopher Sextus Empiricus wrote: "The mills of the gods grind slowly, but they grind small".

Justice may take time, but it will come.

Chapter 23

Fond Farewell

"The key is to keep company with people who uplift you, whose presence calls forth your best" – Epictetus

Dublin, 2015

In June 2015, Scott visited me in Dublin. It was hard to believe it was 25 years since we'd last met up. The bond of our friendship made it seem like a heartbeat. He was touring Europe with stops in Berlin, Paris, Rome, and Madrid. Sadly, he looked tired and dishevelled. From what he told me, he was living listlessly.

His doctors had diagnosed the early stages of Alzheimer's, and it was erasing the blackboard of his life. It was as though he had nurtured a pathological vision of death, and in finding it, he lost sight of all else.

Scott's diagnosis was a salient reminder of the frailty of human health. There's no magic formula in stopping mental degeneration – so much of it is down to luck. Medical experts point to helpful steps in keeping the mind sharp. New experiences - especially shared ones – can give life strength and character, something worth grasping.

Judith Schomaker, assistant professor of neuropsychology at Leiden University in The Netherlands, said that novelty stimulates the brain to create new connections and stay flexible and healthy. Without them, a person's interest in the world lessens and we turn our attention inward, where all neuroses wait patiently.

Scott handed me a photo of the two of us from that epic day on Rottnest Island. It produced a shiver of nostalgia and glee reflected in a quote by American poet and writer Allen Ginsberg, which reads: "The poignancy of a photograph comes from looking back to a fleeting moment in a floating world."

During his five-day stay in Dublin, it was playtime. We dined in fine restaurants and went sight-seeing. I showed him around the city, and he saw the Guinness Storehouse, Grafton Street, St Stephen's Green, and the Book of Kells in Trinity College.

We visited the college's Old Library with its elegant symmetry of wooden alcoves and book-lined galleries stretching up to its domed roof. The awe-inspiring but intimate Long Room is home to some of the world's most valuable ancient books. They give off a mustiness with sweet almondy notes, technically known as a furfural, the pong of decay.

In Oscar Wilde's house on Merrion Square, a guide showed us through the Georgian rooms replete with corniced ceilings, oak floors, mahogany furnishings, and gilt mirrors. Wilde's father, Sir William, was a distinguished eye and ear surgeon. Some medical instruments he invented were on display in the former consultation room.

He was what my dad used to call a 'ladies' man'. He fathered three children before his marriage to Lady Jane, an intellect and poet who spoke a dozen languages. While he recognised his offspring and paid for their education, they were raised by relatives. Both his daughters died in a freakish accident when their dresses caught fire at a party.

On another day, we travelled by Dart train to Howth. As we walked the pier, Scott mentioned to me that the population of Katherine was now over 9,000 and the town even had a McDonald's fast-food restaurant. We later feasted on king scallops and a bottle of Sancerre in the King Sitric.

The next day, boatman Ken Cunningham took us from Coliemore Harbour to Dalkey Island, a place I'd spent many a summer's day as a boy creating memories of idle pleasure.

Scott was impressed by the stately homes along Sorrento and Vico roads. After pointing out the high wooden gates shielding Bono's mansion, we walked up the hill to Killiney village for a pint of Guinness in the Druid's Chair. I told him the pub was once owned by the family of a lifelong friend of mine, Padraic Regan.

After he left Dublin, Scott toured parts of England and Scotland. He was enraptured by the natural beauty of the Cotswolds and the Outer Hebrides. Despite everything, and as always, he said he was content, puzzled by his premature demise, but thankful. He was an old lion. His roar was weaker, but he was still a lion who refused to seek absolution.

Forever stoic, he'd found his paradise in Fremantle. "I'll never leave Freo," he wrote in an email to me shortly before his death in May 2022. "I already live in heaven and when I die, I must stay here." Scott never got to build a better mousetrap, but the generosity he showed to others helped in whatever small way to create a brighter world. His life was enlivened by wonderful memories, despite being marbled with loss.

A tablet in London's Westminster Abbey in memory of William Malcolm Hailey, Lord Hailey of Shahpur, reads: "Mature in youth, youthful in old age. Adorned with grace of wit. Wise, kind, faithful in friendship. In all his dealings, tolerant and humane."

There's no better epitaph for Scott, who deserved to be rewarded with a haven. As another good friend of mine, Justin Feddis, was prone to say when moving on: "If I don't see you round, see you square!"

Chapter 24

Uncharted Waters

Dublin, April 2024

"We have to see the world through a new lens"
– David Attenborough

Australia has not escaped the ravages of climate change, the unprecedented environmental emergency now staring at the world at large. Far from it. The El Nino and La Nina weather patterns have crept into the country's lexicon as the weather becomes more extreme. Climate models determine, broadly, if there will be a hot or a wet summer and indicate the risk of droughts, bushfires, and floods.

The weather patterns were named by fishermen in Peru in the 1600s. Warmer currents off the coast of South America meant fish became scarce, off chasing nutrition-packed cold water. El Nino means 'little boy', named for 'el nino Jesus' as the weather phenomenon peaked at Christmas. A La Nina ('little girl') meant cooler water and fuller nets.

On balance, today's world is hotter during El Nino years. With climate change destabilising the atmosphere and ocean temperatures, we're entering uncharted waters.

An El Nino temporarily disrupts the *status quo* of the Pacific Ocean. The normally cold waters off South America warm up, producing more coastal rain. The waters off Australia get colder, so there's less moisture in the air, lower average rainfall and more of a chance of hot temperatures and bush fires.

As recently as September 2023, the *London Telegraph* reported that the Antarctic's sea-ice had reached a record low, and the consequences could be devastating. Polar experts warned that satellite data showed that Antarctica's sea-ice was way below any previous recorded winter level from March to October.

The continent's area of missing ice is equivalent to almost four times the size of the island of Ireland. "It's so far outside anything we've seen, it's almost mind-blowing," Dr Walter Meier, who monitors sea-ice with the National Snow and Ice Data Centre, said.

Its huge ice expanse regulates the planet's temperature – the white surface reflects the sun's energy back into the atmosphere and cools the water beneath and near it. Without its ice cooling the planet, the frozen realm of Antarctica could transform from Earth's refrigerator to a radiator, experts have said.

Meier told the BBC that he was not optimistic that the sea-ice will recover to a significant degree. The decline in sea-ice kills thousands of emperor penguin chicks every season and is expected to affect other Antarctic species.

Sea ice does not contribute to sea-level rises when it melts. Nevertheless, it does perform a highly important role as a protective buffer on the ice shelves and glaciers on the landmass of Antarctica, to the south of Australasia.

The extent of sea ice remained at record lows during the springtime of 2023.

Dr Robbie Mallet, who is stationed on the Antarctic peninsula, said it is becoming apparent how much more vulnerable the region is to climate change than previously thought. There are "very, very good reasons to be worried," Dr Mallet told the BBC.

"It's potentially an alarming sign of Antarctic climate change that hasn't been there for the last forty years. And it's only emerging now." In 2019, a group of Torres Strait Islanders from low-lying islands off the northern coast of Australia, complained to the United Nations human rights committee about the Australian government, alleging climate inaction.

They asserted that the government had not done enough to reduce emissions or pursue proper adaptation measures on the islands. Consequently, it had failed fundamental human rights obligations to Torres Strait Islander people in terms of their culture and personal freedoms.

One of the complainants, sixth generation Warraber man, Kabay Tamu, said in a statement: "When erosion happens, and the lands get taken away by the seas, it's like a piece of us that gets taken with it – a piece of our heart, a piece of our body. That's why it affects us. Not only the islands but us, as people." In 2022, the UN upheld the islanders' objection.

In 2023, residents of the low-lying Pacific Island nation of Tuvalu were offered the chance to migrate to Australia to escape climate change as part of a landmark treaty with one of countries most affected by global warming. Tuvalu, which lies between Australia and Hawaii, has a population of about 11,000.

The deal allows 280 people affected by rising sea levels to apply for a special visa to resettle in Australia every year. The two countries plan to work together to ensure that there will not be a 'brain drain' from Tuvalu. New Zealand launched a visa scheme in 2017 for Pacific islanders displaced by climate change, but later shelved the plan.

The dominant force in Australian media, Rupert Murdoch's News Corp, continues to promote the use of fossil fuels and gives a platform to the deniers who assiduously ridicule the experts. The Sky News channel is seen as a source for climate science misinformation with soundbites which gain traction among conservative social media influencers and other networks worldwide. Global warming is labelled as a "cult of the elites" and climate emergency as "bogus".

Yet, the effects of climate change are evident right across Australia. Summer beach days in Sydney have been slashed beyond memory by more frequent rain showers and muggy conditions. One theory suggested by climate experts says the influence of El Nina has brought moist air from along the coast of northern Australia, driving wet weather down the eastern seaboard.

Chapter 25

Australia's Own

"The past is never dead. It's not even the past"
– William Faulkner

Dublin, April 2024

Ever since the day Captain James Cook sailed into Sydney Harbour on board Endeavour in 1770, followed by the First Fleet's arrival under Captain Arthur Phillip into Botany Bay in 1788, Australia's Aboriginals had scant fortune in what later became known as 'The Lucky Country'.

The epithet was taken from the title of a book written by Donald Horne in 1964. It became a moniker for Australia around the world. It is normally used favourably, although the phrase's origin was less so in the context of Horne's book. History has underlined their misfortunes.

Lucky? Massive mineral wealth and an outdoor life with all that it brings is one thing. On the flip side, people point to how much of the country's land and mineral wealth was seized by colonisers. They brought with them processed foods, diabetes, cholesterol, and a host of 'white fella' diseases from which the indigenous lifestyle and its close ties with nature had long shielded.

In 1789, a major outbreak of what was widely assumed to have been smallpox wiped out half of the Aboriginal population in Sydney Cove. Thousands of bodies were found lying dead on the beaches and in the caverns of rocks. The colonisers had resistance to smallpox, as they had been exposed to the highly virulent disease back in Europe.

It was suggested that the settlers deliberately brought vials of the smallpox virus to 'ethnically cleanse' and weaken resistance to white settlement. It was not the first time in history that colonisers used biological warfare. In 1763, British soldiers were thought to have given blankets and a handkerchief contaminated with smallpox to Native Americans.

In his book, *This is Not America: Why Black Lives in Britain Matter* (2023), author Tomiwa Owolade wrote that black Americans are the most influential black people in the world. It is not down to the colour of their skin; it is because they are American. Owolade said that the contrast with Indigenous Australians was stark. Traditions are the beating heart of the Aboriginal people, and without which they battle to survive.

In 1901, Australia became a federal nation. Australians were still classified as British citizens and members of the Commonwealth. It was when Chinese immigrants came to Australia to mine gold and taken up work as cane cutters in Queensland and market gardeners in Western Australia. They were poorly treated and often reminded of their allegedly inferior status.

As part of the clampdown on what the country called 'The Yellow Peril', a stop was put to the hiring of Japanese immigrants to dive for pearls off the coast of Broome in northern Western Australia. British divers were brought in as replacement divers, but it soon became clear they were not up to the task. The policy was reversed, and Broome became multi-cultural, and prosperity returned.

At the start of the century, Aboriginals were not recognised as citizens and were actively discriminated against by the State. It set the scene for another 150 years of persecution and domination – a fledgling nation whitewashing the past. Rights activist Vincent Lingiari said: "You can't be mates, you can't be fair dinkum, until you have true equality."

At the opening of Australia's new federal Parliament House in Canberra in May 1927, His Royal Highness the Duke of York, who later became King George VI, was invited to perform the honours amid scenes of "epic pageantry". Over one million Australians listened to the ceremony on radio. Soprano Dame Nellie Melba sang 'God Save the Queen', which was then the country's national anthem.

'Canberra' is an Aboriginal word for 'meeting place' but on that historic day for Australia, the country's Indigenous people were noticeable by their absence. King Billy and Marvellous, two elders of the Wiradjuri community in New South Wales, shocked Australia's political establishment. The two men trekked 200 kilometres from their home to the new capital to raise the issue of sovereignty.

They looked on and refused to leave the new building's forecourt. It was the first recorded instance of Aboriginal protest at parliament. Ever since that day, there have been repeated calls for a statue of King Billy to be erected in Canberra and requests that the trek be recognised as a national march.

On January 26th, 1938, Australia Day, the 150th anniversary of Captain Phillip's arrival into Sydney Harbor's Cove Farm was marked. A re-enactment of the event was planned by the authorities.

When local Aboriginal communities refused to take part, they were told their food rations would end. The organisers were not willing to concede defeat. They brought in men from elsewhere in New South Wales and kept them locked up until it was time for the re-enactment to be staged. On the day itself, the unwilling participants were made to run up the beach away from the British colonisers – an inaccurate version of events.

In 1948, Aboriginals were offered the chance to become citizens along with all other Australians – but with one proviso; they had to give up their traditions and language. Up to this, every Australian was a British citizen. One in six Aboriginal children were adopted by white Australians as part of the Stolen Generation for their "own good".

The scourge of alcohol abuse among Aboriginal communities in the Northern Territory is encapsulated in Film Australia's *Lonely Boy Richard* (2004) documentary, sub-titled *An Intimate Account of One Man's Journey to Jail*. The film presents the human story behind the headlines.

Richard Wanambi battled with alcohol from the age of 14. Years later, he was still drinking heavily and committing crimes. The film shows how night patrols battled on the frontline to bring the drinkers home from the pub in Nhulunbuy and tried their best to keep the 'grog' out of their 'dry' community. The intrusion of the pub and 4,000 white miners in the 1970s changed the community. To this day, Aboriginals pay a hight price for trying to match 'white fellas' in binge drinking sessions in town pubs.

The story also outlines the trials of the Yolyngu people in north-east Arnhem Land – 650 kilometres from Darwin. The Yolngu were the traditional owners of 100,000 square kilometres of land in Yirrkala on the Gove Peninsula for at least 60,000 years.

Yirrkala became a Methodist mission in 1935. In the 1960s, the Australia federal government in Canberra showed an interest in claiming the land for development after it was discovered that the area was rich in bauxite, the raw material used to produce aluminium.

In 1968, the government passed an act granting a 42-year lease to Nabalco, which later became Rio Tinto, the world's second-largest metals and mining company.

The right to mine 300 square kilometres was granted and the destruction of sacred Aboriginal sites went ahead, without any consultation with the Yolngu people. The authorities had chosen to totally ignore the land's rightful owners.

In 1971, the '500 Yolngu of Yirrkala' petitioned the government in the landmark Gove Land Rights court case about mining activity without their consent. It was the first case brought by Aboriginal people which argued that Indigenous Australians should be accepted in law as the rightful owners of their traditional country.

It led to the Commonwealth Aboriginal Land Rights Act of 1976. Under the act, all East Arnhem Land from the mine site to township areas became freehold Aboriginal land. The leases are held by the Northern Land Council (NLC).

When the leases expire in 2053, the land will be given to the Arnhem Aboriginal Land Trust. When mining activity ends, the land will be owned entirely by its traditional owners. In 2011, the Yolngu signed a royalties' agreement with Rio Tinto.

In his rejection of the plaintiff's claims, the presiding judge made the following observation of the Yolngu system of laws: "The evidence shows a subtle and elaborate system highly adapted to the country in which the people led their lives, which provided a stable order of society and was remarkably free from the vagaries of personal whim or influence."

If ever a system could be called 'a government of laws, and not of men', it was shown in the evidence. The judge ruled that Yolngu law was a legal system, but because it did not include proprietorial interests, being the rights to alienate (sell) and to exclude others, it was incapable of being recognised as land law in Australia.

In the early 1970s, the Yolngu began returning to their ancestral lands. They established tiny 'outstation' settlements where they resumed a more traditional lifestyle - hunting, painting, and raising their families away from the temptations and distractions of 'town'.

In 1997, the justice authorities in the Northern Territory introduced mandatory sentencing. Prison numbers almost doubled as adults were jailed for their first offence and juveniles for their second. The hanging of a young boy while in mandatory detention for stealing felt pens sparked national outrage.

Many argued it was evident that Aboriginal people were the targets of this controversial law, in that Aboriginal people had little understanding of 'white laws', least of all the intricacies of mandatory sentencing. In court, most plaintiffs could not understand what was being said, as English was invariably their second if not third language.

Soon after the introduction of mandatory sentencing, Territorians went to the polls and ousted the Country Liberal Party, architects of the zero-tolerance policy. The incoming Labor government immediately repealed mandatory sentencing and introduced its own tough anti-crime legislation. But in effect nothing much changed.

Aboriginal people still appear in court more than white Australians and remain grossly over-represented in prison populations. Jail is not considered shameful or a deterrent as so many men of age spend time behind bars. In some Territory communities, a stint in jail is seen as a rite of passage.

There have been over 500 Indigenous deaths in custody since 1991. Australian journalist and broadcaster John Pilger, who died in December 2023 from pulmonary thrombosis at the age of 84, once described Aboriginals as "the country's people most denied".

In his 2013 film, *Utopia*, Pilger pointed out that almost one in three Aboriginals are dead by the age of 45. The film focused on the Indigenous disadvantage in remote communities, dismantling the Liberal government's basis for its Northern Territory claim of widespread child abuse by Aboriginal men and arguing that "a new Stolen Generation" of indigenous children was emerging.

Pilger remarked: "The whole sorry thing is really to satisfy the white population, not the black population. Until whites give back to blacks their nationhood, they can never claim their own, no matter how many flags they fly." He told the *Guardian* newspaper: "Australia is the land of excuses, not the land of the fair go."

Barrister and Aboriginal activist Professor Mick Dodson said that in recent decades across the Northern Territory, three-quarters of the people behind bars were Aboriginal men. As high as 90 per cent of Aboriginal families are affected by violence. Aboriginal women are 45 times more likely than white women to be victims of violence.

Dodson's claims have been strongly challenged by noted academics and politicians. The fact is that since Australia became a federation of states in 1901, efforts to dispossess and oppress Aboriginals has had a huge adverse impact on their communities.

All children under the age of 21 were made wards of the State. They were removed from their families and sent to missions. Relatives could only visit the children when granted a permit. In June 2022, just over 16 per cent of the country's land area was owned by Aboriginals. Irish immigrants and religious orders took part and benefitted from the oppression.

Dodson, who was voted Australian of the Year in 2009, said human rights do not dispossess people. "Human rights do not marginalise people. They don't cause poverty and gaps in life expectancy and other life outcomes. The value of human rights is not in their existence; it is in their implementation. It's up to us to meet the standards."

He welcomed the national apology made by prime minister Kevin Rudd in 2008. Rudd said "sorry" to the Aboriginal community for past wrongdoings inflicted upon them. It came after over a decade of campaigning by activists for the recognition the victims of the 'Stolen Generations' deserved. "I am inspired by this apology as an act of true reconciliation towards Indigenous Australia," Dodson said in a statement.

Aboriginal athlete and Olympic gold medallist Cathy Freeman said: "I feel there is a real need for (the apology). For my family, it allows some kind of healing and forgiveness to take place where there is less anger and bitterness in the hearts of people."

As prime minister, Liberal leader John Howard had refused to apologise to Indigenous people on the basis that Australians of his generation should not have to accept guilt and blame for past actions and policies over which they had no control.

In 2007, Howard sparked upset among Aboriginal leaders by launching the Northern Territory National Emergency Response, a government action to tackle the alleged abuse of children in Indigenous communities.

New laws saw punitive restrictions on alcohol, imposed conditions on welfare payments and partially suspended race discrimination and land rights acts. Also known as 'The Intervention', the legislation was in place until 2022, when just over 16 per cent of the country's land area was owned by Indigenous Australians.

Maryrose Costello, an MA student at the University of Galway, wrote a module on First Nation Australians in which she noted that even though Aboriginals live in one of the world's wealthiest nations, the statistics for their people are more closely aligned with Third World nations. It was no coincidence but rather it was a result of problems with the commitment to and recognition of Aboriginal culture and needs.

Before Europeans arrived in Australia, there were up to 300 different Aboriginal languages and around 700 different dialects. Many of the languages are no longer used or are under threat. There are now only about fifty Indigenous languages that are 'healthy', in that they are spoken to and used by children.

Aboriginal and Torres Strait Islanders make up 3.8 per cent of Australia's 26 million population. In August 2023, Labor prime minister Anthony Albanese rejected the idea of paying Aboriginals reparations for their treatment by British colonisers. He said that there was no mention of such payments in the Uluru Statement from the Heart. The statement agreed on constitutional recognition and the promise of a better future for the 'First People of Australia'.

Instead, in October 2023, Albanese ran a referendum to recognise Aboriginals in the constitution for the first time through a body called the Voice to Parliament. The motion was defeated with more than 60 per cent of Australians voting no. The country's first referendum in 23 years required a national majority and a majority in at least four states to pass. All six states rejected the proposal.

The proposed body would have been led by Indigenous people who would have advised the government on significant community issues such as health, education, and welfare. In a statement, Aboriginal leaders described the outcome as a "a bitter irony".

Opponents of the referendum, led by the country's major conservative parties, had said throughout the campaign that the proposal would prove divisive. After the vote was defeated, the Yes lobby made the same accusation. They described its rejection as "a shameful act which perpetuates colonialism". It would make the path to reconciliation difficult.

Uncle Eric Law, an elder from a community near Brisbane, said it was a missed opportunity. "I get the impression that the only time white Australia is happy with us is when we have good Aboriginal sports women and men," Law told the *Sydney Morning Herald*. One factor which strongly influenced the outcome of the referendum was a lack of bipartisan support. No referendum has ever been passed in Australia without cross-party backing.

Chapter 26

A Year in Bondi

"If Paris is the city of lights, Sydney is the city of fireworks" – Baz Luhrmann

Julia Cullen, my daughter, recently spent a year in Australia. The final chapter is her story.

Arriving in Sydney at the start of 2023, I had no idea what to expect, aside from gearing myself up to face a cluster of scary spiders and a radical change in weather. Yet even these limited expectations got turned on their head. Fortunately, I only came across one venomous spider throughout the year. I brushed by it as it lay curled up in my Lululemon running shorts on a rainy laundry day in Bondi. Thankfully, it was no harm.

That brings me to my second preconception of Australia: rain. I had imagined that living in New South Wales (NSW), I'd be soaking up the sun on the beach every day. If only. Although the weather is a whole lot better than it is in Ireland, the sky isn't always blue and cloudless - well not in Sydney, anyway. It makes sense as the vastness of the continent allows you to travel across the country and experience wildly, contrasting weather.

During the year, most of my time was spent in Sydney. I was pulled in by the appeal of a vibrant city where many pristine, sandy beaches dotted along the coast are but a stone's throw away. As well as that, my best friend, Nadia Jones, and I first grew our friendship through watching *Bondi Rescue* after school, so it was a kind-of full circle moment to move together across the world and see the pioneers of the surf life-saving movement in the flesh!

Sydney was not all plain sailing. The task of finding a place to live proved trickier than expected. Arriving at viewings with upwards of 50 people in line became the norm. The application process wasn't a doddle either. Along with a month's bond to be paid upfront, Australian landlord and employer references were required.

Quite frankly, trying to find a place to live in Bondi is time-consuming and stressful. Nevertheless, with patience and persistence, it works out in the end. The cost of rent was tough on the wallet but worth it for the quality of life you earn in return.

The energy of Bondi is amazing, with an emphasis on an active and restorative lifestyle. At its southern end is Bondi Baths, an eight-lane, 50-metre saltwater pool built into the cliffs. On my walks along the promenade at 6am, I found myself astonished at the number of people running, swimming, and working out. There's a real sense of accomplishment from starting your day outdoors while the sun is rising.

To stay fit and healthy, people joined one of the many local run clubs. During my time there, I was running with about five clubs a week. From the 440 Club at 4.40am in Bronte to the Coogee Run Club, each has its own vibe to appeal to different people, but they all share the idea of bringing people together to build community and encourage movement. It's easy to get sucked into the 'Bondi Bubble'.

The extent of the Irish community in Sydney surprised me. Such were the numbers of Irish people based in Coogee, the beachside suburb earned the tag 'County Coogee'.

The run clubs allowed me to expand my circle of friends beyond the Irish diaspora and build connections with people from all over the world, from San Francisco to Scotland. The eastern suburbs are more affluent and the cost of living there is higher.

In terms of employment, the sectors offering the most jobs were healthcare and trade. There was plenty of demand for nurses, electricians, and construction workers - 'tradies' and 'leccies'. There were also opportunities in the corporate field. The most difficult aspect about finding a job was making it past the early screening stages.

The eligibility to work in Australia is dependent on a suitable visa. The working holiday visa (WHV) is only valid for twelve months, so there's an additional sponsorship cost to be considered by the hiring team to allow a WHV holder to extend the visa beyond a year. The requirement makes it difficult to stand out against other applicants with full working rights. Like any job hunt, with a bit of patience and perseverance it is possible to find opportunities for both non-citizens and citizens alike.

There was a civic mindedness about Sydneysiders too. One morning, I spotted an airpod in a brown bag left on a pole for rescue by its rightful owner. It was still there days later. A friend from the run club told me about the time he left his laptop on his car roof on busy Hall Street. On his return, four hours later, he was relieved and heartened to find his Mac still in the same place. Local amenities are kept clean and tidy, not least the public toilets and hot showers at the beach.

Sadly, Sydney's reputation as a safe city was shattered by a shocking and tragic incident at Bondi Junction in April 2024. A 40-year-old Queenslander, Joel Cauchi, with a long history of mental illness and whose family said had a fascination with knives, attacked people at the Westfield shopping mall. The man stabbed 18 people, killing six, five of them women.

As in Ireland, violence against women is a growing problem in Australia. More women had been killed by a current or past intimate partner in Australia to date in 2024 than the total number of Australians lost to acts of terror on home soil – ever.

After the 1996 Port Arthur massacre, in which 35 people were killed by a lone gunman, then prime minister John Howard changed the gun laws to ban pump-action, automatic and semi-automatic firearms. One can only imagine what the death toll might have been in Bondi had Cauchi been armed with a gun instead of a knife.

My first visit outside of Sydney was up the east coast to Queensland. The 'Sunshine State' epitomises the weather Irish people associate with Australia - and the further north you go, the more tropical and humid it gets. I played safe and flew into subtropical Byron Bay, a resort popular with hippies, backpackers, and surfers. At the Northern Hotel's Piano Bar, tourists love singing along to the duelling pianists performing requests.

Nadia and I spent a week in Western Australia. We visited vineyards in Margaret River, most especially the Cullen Estate. Back in 1989, my dad and his brother, Peter, met the owner, Dr Kevin Cullen. His six children now run the award-winning winery.

A Year in Bondi

One thing that struck me about Margaret River was the amount of wildlife wandering free. We came across several kangaroos along the open road. The danger for motorists is that if you collide with a 'roo', and it manages to get into your car, they will often punch their way out. One showed up at the door of our Airbnb and was reluctant to leave.

We said hello to the cute and curious quokkas on Rottnest Island. Unlike Sydney, there was no fighting for towel space on the beaches around Perth; they were less explored and peaceful than to what we were used to around Bondi.

It would have been wonderful to have had more time to spend in Western Australia and to have visited my uncle Liam, his wife Gill, and their family. Hearing from my friends who lived there, Perth had its own allure, and in terms of property it was less pricey than Sydney.

I made two trips south to Melbourne; the first to see the city for the first time and meet friends for a St Patrick's Day weekend. The second visit was to spend Christmas with Nadia and her family in Sorrento, a seaside resort with spacious homes and mansions. It reminded me of the Hamptons in New York, an oasis from the hurly-burly of downtown and an ideal place to live life with less demands.

I found people from Melbourne to be amiable and kind to people visiting their city. The city brims with art and culture – it's regarded as Australia's cultural capital – and with good reason. Highlights include the Melbourne Museum and the Australian Centre for Moving Images (ACMI). Both are in Federation Square, just a short walk from the street art on Hozier Lane. The Royal Exhibition Building from 1880 is an architectural gem.

The Department of Home Affairs reported that more than 21,000 young Irish people received WHVs between July 2022 and June 2023 – the highest recorded figure in sixteen years, and double the number recorded for the previous year. The sudden uptick was partly explained by the end of Australia's Covid travel bans.

A total of 48,700 temporary skilled work visas, allowing people to take on certain jobs experiencing domestic skill shortages, were granted to overseas citizens in 2022-2023, an increase of 24,000 on the previous year. Ireland was among the top fifteen countries for securing work visas.

Visas can cost anything between €1,000 and €5,000. As well as that, there are miscellaneous costs for other documents and processes which may be required for visa applications. They include health screens, background checks and occupational skills assessments required for professional qualifications like engineering and nursing outside Australia. Immigration may want to look over a person's bank accounts to ensure they comply with the application.

Shipping household goods to the other side of the world can be expensive too. It is worth investigating whether it makes sense to transport over furniture, electrical and white goods that you had in your home in Ireland. Many retail and online stores in Australia offer similar products at major discounts.

Pet owners need to be aware of quarantine rules and the costs involved. Animals arriving in Australia are quarantined at the country's only facility in Melbourne for between ten and thirty days – it can be up to 180 days if there's an issue. The fee is at the pet owner's expense. A 30-day quarantine can amount to as much as €2,300.

It's as well to have contingency savings should there be a need for an emergency return home. Last-minute flights from Australia to Ireland for one adult can cost up to €3,000 at certain times of the year, like in the run-up to Christmas, so it is something worth keeping in mind when deciding how much might be needed to have set aside in an emergency fund.

For anyone planning to transfer a large amount of savings from Ireland to an Australian bank account, it may be an idea to use services such as Revolut or Wise (formerly known as TransferWise) over international bank transfers, which demand heavy fees and offer less favourable exchange rates. Health insurance cover needs to be addressed too.

Seen in retrospect, Sydney is an exciting place to be during your early to late twenties where you can become part of a bustling community. You can even buy Tayto crisps and Barry's Tea in local supermarkets now. To have spent most of my time in Australia living in Bondi was a joy, with the echoes of memories which I will long treasure.

Printed in Great Britain
by Amazon